THE
GOOD
ENERGY
COOKBOOK

100+ Recipes Inspired by Dr. Casey Means' Expertise to Help You Lose Weight, Boost Wellness, and Maximize Metabolic Health

ELIZA HAYES

TABLE OF CONTENTS

INTRODUCTION

HEALTHY LIFESTYLE

In recent years, the concept of metabolic health has garnered significant attention as research continues to uncover the profound impact it has on our overall well-being. Metabolic health refers to the optimal functioning of the processes that regulate our body's energy production and use, including blood sugar levels, blood pressure, cholesterol, and fat storage. Unfortunately, only a small percentage of adults are metabolically healthy, making this a critical area of focus for anyone interested in improving their health and longevity.

What is Metabolic Health?

Metabolic health is a state in which the body efficiently manages and utilizes energy, ensuring that all biological systems work harmoniously. It's not just about the absence of disease but about maintaining the body in a state of balance where all metabolic processes function optimally. The key markers of metabolic health include stable blood glucose levels, healthy blood pressure, balanced cholesterol levels, appropriate waist circumference, and optimal triglyceride levels. When these markers are within healthy ranges, the risk of chronic diseases such as type 2 diabetes, heart disease, and stroke is significantly reduced.

1. Key Markers of Metabolic Health

- **Blood Glucose Levels:** Blood glucose, or blood sugar, is the primary energy source for the body's cells. Stable blood glucose levels are crucial for preventing insulin resistance, which can lead to type 2 diabetes. Ideally, fasting blood glucose levels should be below 100 mg/dL, and HbA1c levels (which measure average blood sugar over three months) should be below 5.7%.

- **Blood Pressure:** Healthy blood pressure is essential for reducing the risk of heart disease and stroke. Blood pressure is considered normal when it is below 120/80 mm Hg. High blood pressure can damage blood vessels and increase the risk of atherosclerosis, a condition where arteries become narrowed and hardened, leading to cardiovascular complications.

- **Cholesterol Levels:** Cholesterol, while necessary for building cells and producing hormones, must be kept in balance. HDL (high-density lipoprotein) is the "good" cholesterol that helps remove other forms of cholesterol from your bloodstream.Low density lipoprotein (LDL) is "bad" cholesterol that can build up in the walls of your arteries.Maintaining high levels of HDL and low levels of LDL is crucial for heart health. Total cholesterol levels should be below 200 mg/dL, with LDL levels below 100 mg/dL and HDL levels above 60 mg/dL.

- **Waist Circumference:** Waist circumference is a simple measure of abdominal fat, which is a key indicator of metabolic health. Excess abdominal fat is strongly linked to insulin resistance, inflammation, and cardiovascular disease. A healthy waist circumference is generally less than 40 inches for men and less than 35 inches for women.

- **Triglyceride Levels:** Triglycerides are a form of fat present in your bloodstream. High levels of triglycerides can increase the risk of heart disease. Normal triglyceride levels should be below 150 mg/dL. Elevated triglycerides often occur alongside other conditions like high blood pressure and obesity, collectively known as metabolic syndrome.

1. Beyond Weight: Understanding True Metabolic Health

Understanding metabolic health is essential because it goes beyond merely maintaining a healthy weight. A person can appear to be in good shape on the outside but still suffer from poor metabolic health internally. This internal imbalance often leads to symptoms such as fatigue, brain fog, hormonal imbalances, and, eventually, chronic illness. Thus, achieving metabolic health is not just about looking good; it's about feeling good and ensuring the body functions at its best.

Metabolic health is intricately linked to how efficiently your body processes and utilizes energy. Even individuals with a normal body mass index (BMI) can experience metabolic dysregulation if their diet is poor or if they lead a sedentary lifestyle. This phenomenon, often referred to as "TOFI" (thin outside, fat inside), highlights the importance of looking beyond weight and focusing on overall metabolic function.

The Importance of Glucose Regulation

Glucose regulation plays a pivotal role in metabolic health. Glucose, derived from the carbohydrates in our diet, is the primary energy source for our cells. However, maintaining balanced blood sugar levels is crucial for avoiding metabolic disorders. When we consume foods high in refined sugars or simple carbohydrates, they cause rapid spikes in blood glucose. The pancreas then releases insulin to lower blood sugar levels by facilitating the storage of excess glucose as fat.

1. Understanding Insulin and its Role

Insulin is a hormone produced by the pancreas that allows cells to absorb glucose from the blood for energy or storage. When you consume food, carbohydrates are converted into glucose, which then enters your bloodstream. In response, the pancreas releases insulin, which signals cells to take in glucose. This process keeps blood glucose levels within a narrow range, ensuring that the body has a steady energy supply while preventing hyperglycemia (high blood sugar).

However, chronic consumption of high-glycemic foods can lead to a condition known as insulin resistance. In insulin resistance, the body's cells become less responsive to insulin, requiring more insulin to achieve the same effect. Over time, the pancreas struggles to produce enough insulin, leading to higher blood glucose levels and eventually type 2 diabetes. Insulin resistance is a key component of metabolic syndrome, a cluster of conditions that significantly increase the risk of heart disease, stroke, and diabetes.

2. The Dangers of Chronic Blood Sugar Spikes

Chronic blood sugar spikes and crashes can have serious consequences for metabolic health. Frequent spikes in blood sugar levels cause repeated insulin release, which can lead to insulin resistance. Additionally, blood sugar crashes, or hypoglycemia, can result in symptoms such as shakiness, fatigue, irritability, and cravings for more high-sugar foods, perpetuating a vicious cycle.

Beyond insulin resistance, chronic high blood sugar can damage blood vessels and nerves, leading to complications such as neuropathy, kidney disease, and retinopathy (eye damage). It also contributes to the formation of advanced glycation end-products (AGEs), which accelerate aging and increase the risk of chronic diseases.

3. Strategies for Maintaining Stable Blood Sugar Levels

To maintain optimal glucose levels, it's important to focus on a diet rich in complex carbohydrates, lean proteins, and healthy fats. Foods with a low glycemic index (GI), which cause slower, more controlled increases in blood sugar, are particularly beneficial. The glycemic index ranks foods based on how they affect blood glucose levels. Low-GI foods, such as non-starchy vegetables, legumes, and whole grains, provide a slow, steady release of glucose into the bloodstream, preventing spikes and crashes.

Incorporating fiber-rich foods into your diet is another effective strategy. Fiber slows down the digestion and absorption of carbohydrates, resulting in more gradual increases in blood sugar. Foods high in fiber, such as vegetables, fruits, and whole grains, are also more filling, helping to control appetite and prevent overeating.

Balanced meals that include a mix of protein, healthy fats, and complex carbohydrates can further help stabilize blood sugar levels. Protein and fat slow down the digestion of carbohydrates, reducing the likelihood of rapid blood sugar spikes. Additionally, regular physical activity, adequate hydration, and stress management are crucial for maintaining insulin sensitivity and overall glucose regulation.

How Foods Affect Our Health

What we eat directly impacts our metabolic health. Nutrient-dense foods like vegetables, whole grains, lean proteins, and healthy fats support the body's ability to regulate blood sugar, maintain a healthy weight, and protect against inflammation. Conversely, processed foods high in sugars, unhealthy fats, and refined grains can disrupt glucose regulation and lead to chronic inflammation, contributing to a host of metabolic disorders.

1. The Role of Macronutrients in Metabolic Health

Macronutrients—carbohydrates, proteins, and fats—are the primary components of our diet and each plays a distinct role in metabolic health.

- **Carbohydrates:** Carbohydrates serve as the primary fuel for the body. However, the type of carbohydrate consumed matters significantly. Simple carbohydrates, found in sugary foods and refined grains, are quickly broken down into glucose, leading to rapid spikes in blood sugar. In contrast, complex carbohydrates, such as those in whole grains, legumes, and vegetables, are digested more slowly, providing a steady supply of energy and maintaining stable blood sugar levels.

- **Proteins:** Protein is crucial for tissue repair and growth, the production of enzymes and hormones, and maintaining a healthy immune system. This can also contribute to regulating blood sugar by slowing down the absorption of carbohydrates. High-protein foods such as lean meats, fish, eggs, and legumes can help maintain satiety, prevent overeating, and support muscle mass, which is important for maintaining a healthy metabolism.

- **Fats:** Healthy fats, such as those found in avocados, nuts, seeds, and olive oil, are crucial for brain health, hormone production, and the absorption of fat-soluble vitamins (A, D, E, K). Fats also provide a slow-burning energy source that can help stabilize blood sugar levels and keep you feeling full for longer periods.

2. The Importance of Micronutrients

Beyond macronutrients, micronutrients—vitamins and minerals—also play a crucial role in metabolic health. Micronutrients such as magnesium, chromium, and B vitamins are essential for glucose metabolism. For example:

- **Magnesium:** This mineral plays a vital role in over 300 biochemical reactions in the body, including glucose regulation. Magnesium helps insulin function properly and supports glucose uptake by cells. Foods rich in magnesium include leafy green vegetables, nuts, seeds, and whole grains.
- **Chromium:** Chromium is involved in carbohydrate and lipid metabolism and helps enhance the action of insulin. It's found in foods such as broccoli, potatoes, whole grains, and lean meats.
- **B Vitamins:** B vitamins, particularly B6, B12, and folate, are important for energy production, DNA synthesis, and red blood cell formation. They also play a role in regulating homocysteine levels, an amino acid linked to heart disease. Good sources of B vitamins include whole grains, meat, eggs, dairy products, and leafy greens.

A diet deficient in these and other essential nutrients can impair the body's ability to manage blood sugar, leading to metabolic imbalance. It's important to consume a varied diet that includes a wide range of nutrient-rich foods to ensure adequate intake of all essential vitamins and minerals.

3. Gut Health and Its Impact on Metabolism

Gut health is another critical factor in metabolic health. The gut microbiome, a complex community of trillions of microorganisms living in the digestive tract, plays a vital role in digestion, nutrient absorption, immune function, and even mood regulation. Emerging research suggests that the gut microbiome also has a significant impact on metabolic health.

A healthy gut microbiome supports efficient digestion and nutrient absorption, which in turn supports overall metabolic function. For example, certain gut bacteria help break down dietary fiber into short-chain fatty acids (SCFAs), which are absorbed into the bloodstream and used as energy. SCFAs also have anti-inflammatory effects and may help regulate blood sugar and appetite.

Conversely, an imbalanced gut microbiome, often characterized by a lack of diversity and an overgrowth of harmful bacteria, has been linked to obesity, insulin resistance, and other metabolic disorders. Diet plays a crucial role in shaping the gut microbiome. A diet rich in fiber, fermented foods, and prebiotics (foods that feed beneficial bacteria) supports a healthy and diverse gut microbiome, while a diet high in processed foods, sugars, and unhealthy fats can disrupt it.

Introduction to Metabolic Cooking

Metabolic cooking is about creating meals that support stable blood sugar levels, optimize energy production, and promote overall health. The recipes in this book focus on whole, unprocessed ingredients that are nutrient-dense and low on the glycemic index. You'll learn how to prepare meals that are not only delicious but also designed to support your metabolic health.

1. Principles of Metabolic Cooking

The key principles of metabolic cooking include:

- **Nutrient Density:** Focus on ingredients that provide a high amount of vitamins, minerals, and other beneficial compounds relative to their calorie content. Nutrient-dense foods support overall health and help maintain metabolic balance.

- **Low Glycemic Index:** Choose foods that have a low glycemic index to prevent rapid spikes in blood sugar. This includes incorporating whole grains, legumes, vegetables, and fruits that are digested slowly and provide sustained energy.

- **Balanced Macronutrients:** Create meals that balance carbohydrates, proteins, and fats. This equilibrium aids in maintaining stable blood sugar levels, enhances feelings of fullness, and supports metabolic function.

- **Healthy Fats:** Include sources of healthy fats, such as olive oil, nuts, seeds, and avocados. These fats are essential for hormone production, brain health, and energy.

- **Fiber-Rich Foods:** Incorporate a variety of fiber-rich vegetables, fruits, and whole grains to support digestion, promote satiety, and regulate blood sugar levels.

2. Cooking Techniques for Metabolic Health

Metabolic cooking isn't just about the ingredients; it's also about how you prepare them. The right cooking techniques can preserve nutrients, enhance flavor, and promote health. Some techniques include:

- **Steaming:** Preserves the nutrients in vegetables better than boiling and avoids the addition of unhealthy fats.

- **Roasting:** Brings out the natural sweetness in vegetables and can be done with minimal oil, making it a healthier alternative to frying.

- **Grilling:** Adds flavor to meats and vegetables without the need for heavy sauces or fats.

- **Sautéing:** A quick cooking method that retains nutrients in vegetables when done with healthy oils like olive or avocado oil.

3. The Role of Spices and Herbs

Spices and herbs not only enhance the flavor of your meals but also offer numerous health benefits. For example, turmeric has anti-inflammatory properties, cinnamon can help regulate blood sugar levels, and garlic has been shown to improve heart health. Metabolic cooking encourages the use of these natural flavor enhancers to create meals that are both delicious and health-promoting.

4. Meal Planning and Preparation

To make metabolic cooking sustainable, meal planning and preparation are essential. By planning your meals ahead of time, you can ensure that you always have healthy options available, reducing the temptation to reach for processed or unhealthy foods. Batch cooking, freezing portions, and preparing ingredients in advance are all strategies that can help you stick to your metabolic health goals.

HOW TO USE THIS BOOK

Embarking on a journey to better metabolic health can be both exciting and overwhelming. This cookbook is designed to be your guide, providing not only delicious recipes but also the knowledge and tools you need to make informed choices about your diet and lifestyle. To get the most out of this book, it's important to understand how it is structured and how you can tailor it to your personal needs and goals. By doing so, you can make the transition to healthier eating habits more enjoyable and sustainable, ensuring that the positive changes you make are long-lasting.

Structure of the Book

This cookbook is meticulously organized into several key sections, each designed to support different aspects of your metabolic health journey. Understanding the structure of the book will help you navigate through the content efficiently and make the most of the resources provided.

1. Introduction to Metabolic Health

The book begins with an in-depth introduction to metabolic health, which serves as the foundation for everything that follows. This section explains the science behind how food impacts your body's ability to regulate blood sugar, maintain energy levels, and prevent chronic disease. By gaining a solid understanding of these principles, you'll be better equipped to make informed decisions about your diet and how it affects your overall health.

This introduction also addresses the key concepts of metabolic health, such as insulin sensitivity, glycemic index, and the role of macronutrients and micronutrients. It's designed to demystify complex nutritional science, making it accessible and applicable to your daily life. The goal is to empower you with knowledge so that you can confidently apply the principles of metabolic health in your cooking and eating habits.

2. Recipe Chapters

The core of the book is divided into chapters based on meal types: breakfast, lunch, dinner, snacks, and desserts. Each chapter is curated to provide a variety of recipes that cater to different tastes, dietary preferences, and nutritional needs, all while supporting metabolic health.

- **Breakfast:** This chapter emphasizes the importance of starting your day with a balanced meal that provides sustained energy. The recipes focus on nutrient-dense ingredients that are low on the glycemic index, helping to stabilize blood sugar levels after the overnight fast.

- **Lunch:** Lunch recipes are designed to be satisfying yet light enough to prevent afternoon energy crashes. They include a mix of lean proteins, whole grains, and vegetables, offering a balance of macronutrients that will keep you full and focused throughout the day.

- **Dinner:** Dinner is an opportunity to wind down with a meal that nourishes your body without overloading it. The recipes in this chapter focus on lean proteins, healthy fats, and a generous serving of vegetables, promoting restful sleep and recovery.

- **Snacks:** Healthy snacking is crucial for maintaining steady energy levels between meals. This chapter offers a variety of snack options that are quick to prepare, portable, and designed to curb hunger without causing blood sugar spikes.

- **Desserts:** Yes, you can enjoy desserts while maintaining metabolic health! The dessert recipes in this chapter use natural sweeteners, low-glycemic ingredients, and portion control to satisfy your sweet tooth without derailing your health goals.

3. Make-Ahead Meals

For those with busy schedules, the make-ahead meals chapter is a lifesaver. This section is dedicated to recipes that can be prepared in advance, making it easier to stick to your nutritional goals even on the busiest of days. These meals are designed to be stored and reheated without losing their flavor or nutritional value.

Make-ahead meals are particularly beneficial for maintaining metabolic health because they prevent last-minute, unhealthy food choices. By having healthy options readily available, you can avoid the temptation of processed foods and fast food, which are often high in sugars, unhealthy fats, and empty calories.

4. Weekly Meal Plan

To simplify your meal planning, the book includes a comprehensive weekly meal plan. This plan is designed to be a flexible guide, helping you create balanced meals that support your metabolic health throughout the week. Each day includes a breakfast, lunch, and dinner, along with optional snacks and desserts. The meals are balanced to maintain steady blood sugar levels, prevent energy crashes, and keep you feeling satisfied.

The meal plan is accompanied by a detailed shopping list that includes all the ingredients you'll need for the week. This list is designed to make your grocery shopping as efficient as possible, saving you time and reducing food waste.

The meal plan can also serve as inspiration. If you prefer more variety or have specific dietary needs, you can mix and match recipes from the book to create your own personalized plan. Whether you follow the meal plan exactly or use it as a starting point, it's there to make healthy eating easier and more manageable.

Tips for Using the Recipes

While the recipes in this book are designed to be straightforward and accessible, there are a few tips that can help you get the most out of them. These tips will not only enhance your cooking experience but also ensure that the meals you prepare are aligned with your personal health goals.

1. Start with the Basics

If you're new to metabolic cooking, begin with the simpler recipes to build your confidence. Starting with basic recipes allows you to familiarize yourself with new ingredients and cooking techniques without feeling overwhelmed. As you become more comfortable in the kitchen, you can experiment with more complex dishes, gradually expanding your culinary skills and repertoire.

For example, you might start with a basic breakfast smoothie or a simple grilled chicken salad. These recipes are easy to prepare, require minimal ingredients, and provide a great introduction to the principles of metabolic cooking. Once you've mastered the basics, you can move on to more elaborate meals, such as a baked fish dish with a complex spice blend or a vegetable stir-fry with homemade sauce.

2. Personalize Your Meals

Every individual's metabolic needs are different, and it's important to tailor the recipes to suit your personal preferences, dietary restrictions, or metabolic goals. Don't hesitate to adjust recipes based on what works best for you. For instance, if you have a gluten intolerance, you can swap out wheat flour for almond flour or coconut flour. If you're vegetarian or vegan, many recipes can be adapted by substituting animal proteins with plant-based alternatives like tofu, tempeh, or legumes.

Personalization also extends to portion sizes. Depending on your activity level, weight management goals, and metabolic rate, you may need to adjust the portions of proteins, fats, and carbohydrates in each meal. The flexibility of these recipes allows you to customize them in a way that best supports your health.

Additionally, you can modify recipes to align with specific health objectives. For example, if you're focusing on weight loss, you might reduce the amount of fat or carbohydrates in a recipe while increasing the protein content. Conversely, if you're aiming to build muscle, you might want to increase the portion size or add more protein-rich ingredients.

3. Focus on Freshness

Whenever possible, use fresh, whole ingredients. Fresh vegetables, fruits, and proteins are not only more nutrient-dense but also offer better flavor, making your meals both healthier and more enjoyable. Fresh ingredients are less likely to contain added sugars, unhealthy fats, and preservatives, which can negatively impact metabolic health.

Shopping for fresh produce regularly, ideally from local farmers' markets, can enhance the quality of your meals. Local, seasonal produce is often fresher, more flavorful, and higher in nutrients compared to out-of-season items that have traveled long distances.

In addition to vegetables and fruits, focus on sourcing high-quality proteins and fats. Choose grass-fed meats, wild-caught fish, and organic eggs when possible. These options are generally richer in omega-3 fatty acids and lower in harmful additives than their conventionally raised counterparts.

4. Meal Prep for Success

Consider setting aside time each week to prep ingredients or cook meals in advance. Meal prepping can make it easier to stick to your nutritional goals, especially on busy days when you might otherwise be tempted to reach for less healthy options.

Meal prep might involve batch cooking a large portion of a recipe and storing it in individual servings for the week. It could also include pre-chopping vegetables, marinating proteins, or preparing grains in advance so that assembling a meal takes only a few minutes.

For example, you might prepare a large batch of quinoa and grilled chicken on the weekend, which can be used throughout the week in salads, bowls, or wraps. Having these components ready to go reduces the effort required to make a healthy meal and ensures that you have nutritious options available at all times.

Additionally, meal prepping can help you manage portion sizes more effectively. By dividing meals into individual containers, you can prevent overeating and ensure that you're consuming the right amount of food for your metabolic needs.

Understanding the Meal Plan

The meal plan provided in this book is designed to be a flexible guide, helping you create balanced meals that support your metabolic health throughout the week. Each day includes a breakfast, lunch, and dinner, along with optional snacks and desserts. The meals are balanced to maintain steady blood sugar levels, prevent energy crashes, and keep you feeling satisfied.

1. Customizing the Meal Plan

If you have specific health goals, such as weight loss, muscle gain, or managing a chronic condition like diabetes, you can modify the meal plan to better suit your needs. For instance, you might adjust portion sizes to control calorie intake, focus on lower-carb recipes if you're managing blood sugar, or include more protein-rich meals to support muscle growth.

The meal plan is designed to be a starting point. Feel free to mix and match recipes from different days, substitute ingredients based on what you have available, or add extra snacks if needed. The flexibility of the plan allows you to adapt it to your lifestyle and preferences, making it easier to stick to in the long run.

2. The Role of Snacks and Desserts

Snacks and desserts are included in the meal plan to ensure that you have options for satisfying hunger between meals and indulging your sweet tooth in a healthy way. These snacks and desserts are carefully crafted to be low in sugars and unhealthy fats while providing essential nutrients.

For example, a snack might consist of a handful of nuts and a piece of fruit, which offers a balance of healthy fats, fiber, and natural sugars to keep you energized between meals. Desserts might include options like chia seed pudding or a small serving of dark chocolate, which can satisfy cravings without spiking blood sugar levels.

By including snacks and desserts in your meal plan, you can prevent the deprivation that often leads to overeating or making unhealthy choices. Instead, you'll have a steady supply of nutritious foods that keep you satisfied throughout the day.

3. Making Adjustments Based on Progress

As you follow the meal plan, it's important to monitor your progress and make adjustments as needed. Pay attention to how your body responds to the meals—whether you feel energized, satisfied, and comfortable with the portions. If you find that certain meals leave you feeling hungry or overly full, don't hesitate to tweak the plan.

For instance, if you notice that you're hungry shortly after breakfast, you might need to increase the protein or fiber content of that meal. Alternatively, if you're finding it difficult to finish the portions at dinner, consider reducing the serving size or saving part of the meal for the next day.

The key is to listen to your body and adjust the plan to meet your needs. This personalized approach will help you maintain a healthy relationship with food and achieve your metabolic health goals more effectively.

Tools and Ingredients

To make the most of the recipes in this book, you'll want to have some basic kitchen tools and staple ingredients on hand. These tools and ingredients will help you prepare meals efficiently and effectively, ensuring that you can follow the recipes with ease and achieve the best results.

1. Essential Kitchen Tools

Having the right tools in your kitchen can make a significant difference in your cooking experience. The following tools are recommended for preparing the recipes in this book:

- **Sharp Knife and Cutting Board:** A high-quality chef's knife and a sturdy cutting board are essential for chopping vegetables, slicing meats, and preparing ingredients efficiently. A sharp knife not only makes the task easier but also safer.

- **Blender:** A blender is useful for making smoothies, soups, and sauces. If possible, invest in a high-powered blender that can handle tough ingredients like nuts and seeds.

- **Food Processor:** A food processor can save you time when chopping vegetables, making doughs, or blending ingredients for dips and spreads. It's especially useful for recipes that require finely chopped or pureed ingredients.

- **Various Cooking Pans:** A set of non-stick or stainless-steel pans in different sizes will allow you to sauté, fry, and simmer ingredients with ease. Consider having a large skillet, a medium saucepan, and a small frying pan on hand.

- **Baking Sheets and Pans:** For recipes that require baking or roasting, a selection of baking sheets and pans is essential. Make sure to have a few sizes available, including a standard baking sheet, a loaf pan, and a muffin tin.

- **Measuring Cups and Spoons:** Accurate measurements are crucial for following recipes correctly. Invest in a good set of measuring cups and spoons to ensure that you're using the right amounts of ingredients.

- **Mixing Bowls:** A set of mixing bowls in various sizes will come in handy for preparing and combining ingredients. Stainless steel or glass bowls are durable and easy to clean.

- **Storage Containers:** To make meal prep easier, have a collection of airtight storage containers in different sizes. These are useful for storing leftovers, portioning meals, and keeping prepped ingredients fresh.

2. Stocking Your Pantry

The recipes in this book rely on whole, minimally processed foods, so it's important to keep your pantry stocked with staple ingredients that you can use to prepare healthy meals at any time. Here are some key items to have on hand:

- **Healthy Fats:** Olive oil, coconut oil, avocado oil, and ghee are excellent sources of healthy fats for cooking and dressing salads.

- **Nuts and Seeds:** Almonds, walnuts, chia seeds, flaxseeds, and sunflower seeds are versatile ingredients that can be used in smoothies, salads, snacks, and baking.

- **Whole Grains:** Stock up on whole grains like quinoa, brown rice, oats, and barley. These offer a consistent supply of complex carbohydrates and dietary fiber.

- **Legumes:** Beans, lentils, and chickpeas are rich in protein, fiber, and essential nutrients. Keep dried or canned legumes in your pantry for easy addition to soups, stews, and salads.

- **Spices and Herbs:** A well-stocked spice rack is essential for adding flavor and health benefits to your meals. Some basics include turmeric, cumin, paprika, cinnamon, oregano, basil, and rosemary.

- **Vinegars and Condiments:** Apple cider vinegar, balsamic vinegar, soy sauce (or tamari for a gluten-free option), and mustard are versatile condiments that can enhance the flavor of many dishes.

- **Natural Sweeteners:** Instead of refined sugar, use natural sweeteners like honey, maple syrup, and stevia. These can be used in moderation to add sweetness to recipes without spiking blood sugar levels.

- **Canned Goods:** Canned tomatoes, coconut milk, and broth are convenient staples that can be used in a variety of recipes. Seek out choices that contain no added sugars or preservatives.

3. Fresh Ingredients

In addition to pantry staples, it's important to keep your kitchen stocked with fresh ingredients that can be used in your daily meals. Focus on seasonal produce, lean proteins, and dairy or dairy alternatives:

- **Vegetables:** Fresh, seasonal vegetables should be the cornerstone of your meals. Leafy greens, cruciferous vegetables (like broccoli and cauliflower), bell peppers, tomatoes, and zucchini are all nutrient-dense options.

- **Fruits:** Keep a variety of fresh fruits on hand for snacks, smoothies, and desserts. Berries, apples, bananas, and citrus fruits are all great options.

- **Lean Proteins:** Chicken, turkey, fish, eggs, and tofu are versatile protein sources that can be used in a wide range of recipes. If possible, choose organic, free-range, or wild-caught options.

- **Dairy and Alternatives:** Depending on your dietary preferences, keep a supply of dairy or plant-based alternatives in your fridge. Greek yogurt, almond milk, and cheese are all great options.

By having these tools and ingredients readily available, you'll be well-prepared to tackle any recipe in this book. Whether you're whipping up a quick breakfast or preparing a gourmet dinner, the right tools and ingredients will make the process smoother and more enjoyable.

CHAPTER 1
BREAKFAST FOR A GREAT START

Green Smoothie with Spinach and Avocado

2

10 Minutes

/

INGREDIENTS

- 2 cups fresh spinach leaves
- 1 ripe avocado, peeled and pitted
- 1 banana
- 1 cup unsweetened almond milk
- 1 tablespoon chia seeds
- 1 tablespoon honey or
- maple syrup (optional)
- 1/2 cup ice cubes

INSTRUCTIONS

1. In a blender, add the spinach, avocado, banana, and almond milk.
2. Blend until smooth.
3. Add the chia seeds, honey or maple syrup (if using), and ice cubes.
4. Blend again until all ingredients are well combined and smooth.
5. Pour into glasses and serve immediately

Almond Flour Pancakes with Berries

4

10 Minutes

20 Minutes

INGREDIENTS

- 1 cup almond flour
- 1/4 teaspoon baking soda
- 1/4 teaspoon salt
- 2 large eggs
- 1/4 cup unsweetened almond milk
- 1 tablespoon maple syrup
- 1 teaspoon vanilla extract
- 1 tablespoon coconut oil (for cooking)
- 1 cup mixed berries (blueberries, strawberries, raspberries)

INSTRUCTIONS

1. In a bowl, mix almond flour, baking soda, and salt.
2. In a separate bowl, whisk together eggs, almond milk, maple syrup, and vanilla extract.
3. Mix the wet and dry ingredients together until the mixture is smooth.
4. Heat a non-stick skillet over medium heat and add a little coconut oil.
5. Pour about 1/4 cup of the batter onto the skillet for each pancake.
6. Cook for 2-3 minutes on each side, until golden brown.
7. Serve pancakes warm with mixed berries on top.

Scrambled Eggs with Spinach and Avocado

 2

 5 Minutes

 5 Minutes

INGREDIENTS

- 4 large eggs
- 1/4 cup milk or cream
- Salt and pepper, to taste
- 1 tablespoon butter
- 1 cup fresh spinach leaves
- 1 ripe avocado, sliced

INSTRUCTIONS

1. In a bowl, whisk together the eggs, milk or cream, salt, and pepper.
2. Heat butter in a non-stick skillet over medium heat.
3. Add the spinach and cook until wilted, about 1-2 minutes.
4. Pour the egg mixture into the skillet and cook, stirring frequently, until scrambled and fully cooked.
5. Serve scrambled eggs with sliced avocado on the side.

Chia Seed Porridge with Almond Milk

 2

5 Minutes

Soaking Time 4 hours or overnight

INGREDIENTS

- 1/4 cup chia seeds
- 1 cup unsweetened almond milk
- 1 tablespoon honey or maple syrup
- 1/2 teaspoon vanilla extract
- Fresh fruit, nuts, or seeds for topping

INSTRUCTIONS

1. In a bowl, combine chia seeds, almond milk, honey or maple syrup, and vanilla extract.
2. Stir well and let sit for about 10 minutes, stirring occasionally.
3. Cover and refrigerate for at least 4 hours or overnight to thicken.
4. Before serving, stir the porridge again and add more almond milk if needed to achieve desired consistency.
5. Top with fresh fruit, nuts, or seeds, and serve.

Mushroom and Fresh Herbs Omelette

INGREDIENTS

1

5 minutes

10 minutes

- 2 large eggs
- 1 tablespoon milk or water
- Salt and pepper, to taste
- 1 tablespoon butter
- 1/2 cup sliced mushrooms
- 1 tablespoon chopped fresh herbs (parsley, chives, thyme)

INSTRUCTIONS

1. In a bowl, whisk together the eggs, milk or water, salt, and pepper.
2. Heat butter in a non-stick skillet over medium heat.
3. Add the mushrooms and sauté until softened, about 3-4 minutes.
4. Pour the egg mixture over the mushrooms in the skillet.
5. Cook without stirring for 1-2 minutes, until the edges start to set.
6. Sprinkle the fresh herbs over the eggs.
7. Fold the omelette in half and cook for another minute or until fully set.
8. Serve warm.

Homemade Granola with Nuts and Seeds

6

10 Minutes

25 Minutes

INGREDIENTS

- 2 cups rolled oats
- 1/2 cup almonds, chopped
- 1/2 cup walnuts, chopped
- 1/4 cup sunflower seeds
- 1/4 cup pumpkin seeds
- 1/4 cup honey or maple syrup
- 1/4 cup coconut oil, melted
- 1 teaspoon vanilla extract
- 1/2 teaspoon ground cinnamon
- Pinch of salt

INSTRUCTIONS

1. Preheat your oven to 325°F (160°C).
2. In a large bowl, combine oats, almonds, walnuts, sunflower seeds, and pumpkin seeds.
3. In a separate bowl, mix honey or maple syrup, coconut oil, vanilla extract, cinnamon, and salt.
4. Pour the wet ingredients over the dry ingredients and stir until evenly coated.
5. Spread the mixture onto a baking sheet lined with parchment paper.
6. Bake for 20-25 minutes, stirring halfway through, until golden brown.
7. Let cool completely before storing in an airtight container.

Zucchini and Pepper Frittata

 4

 10 minutes

 20 minutes

INGREDIENTS

- 1 tablespoon olive oil
- 1 small onion, diced
- 1 zucchini, thinly sliced
- 1 red bell pepper, diced
- 6 large eggs
- 1/4 cup milk
- Salt and pepper, to taste
- 1/4 cup grated Parmesan cheese (optional)

INSTRUCTIONS

1. Preheat your oven to 350°F (175°C).
2. Heat olive oil in an oven-safe skillet over medium heat.
3. Add the onion and sauté for approximately 3 minutes, or until it becomes soft.
4. Add zucchini and bell pepper, cooking for another 5 minutes until vegetables are tender.
5. In a bowl, whisk together eggs, milk, salt, and pepper.
6. Pour the egg mixture into the skillet over the vegetables.
7. Cook on the stove for 2-3 minutes, then transfer the skillet to the oven.
8. Bake for 15 minutes or until the frittata is set.
9. If you like, sprinkle Parmesan cheese on top before serving.

Baked Egg and Vegetable Muffins

 6 muffins

 10 minutes

20 minutes

INGREDIENTS

- 6 large eggs
- 1/4 cup milk
- Salt and pepper, to taste
- 1/2 cup chopped spinach
- 1/2 cup diced bell peppers
- 1/4 cup diced onion
- 1/4 cup shredded cheese (optional)

INSTRUCTIONS

1. Preheat your oven to 375°F (190°C).
2. Coat a muffin tin with cooking spray or a bit of oil.
3. In a bowl, beat the eggs, milk, salt, and pepper together with a whisk.
4. Add the spinach, bell peppers, and onion to the egg mixture, stirring to combine.
5. Pour the mixture evenly into the muffin cups.
6. Sprinkle with cheese if desired.
7. Bake for 18-20 minutes, until the eggs are fully set.
8. Let cool before removing from the muffin tin.

Greek Yogurt with Nuts and Honey

2

5 minutes

/

- 2 cups Greek yogurt
- 1/4 cup mixed nuts (almonds, walnuts, pistachios), chopped
- 2 tablespoons honey
- Fresh fruit (optional)

INSTRUCTIONS

1. Divide the Greek yogurt between two bowls.
2. Top each bowl with chopped nuts.
3. Drizzle honey over the yogurt and nuts.
4. Add fresh fruit on top, if desired.
5. Serve immediately.

Whole Grain Toast with Avocado and Sesame Seeds

2

5 Minutes

2 Minutes

INGREDIENTS

- 4 slices whole grain bread
- 2 ripe avocados
- Salt and pepper, to taste
- 1 tablespoon sesame seeds
- Red pepper flakes (optional)

INSTRUCTIONS

1. Toast the slices of whole grain bread to your desired level of crispiness.
2. While the bread is toasting, cut the avocados in half, remove the pit, and scoop out the flesh into a bowl.
3. Mash the avocado with a fork, adding salt and pepper to taste.
4. Spread the mashed avocado evenly onto the toasted bread slices.
5. Sprinkle with sesame seeds and red pepper flakes, if using.
6. Serve immediately.

CHAPTER 2
NUTRIENT-DENSE AND SATISFYING LUNCHES

Quinoa Salad with Avocado, Tomatoes, and Black Beans

4

15 Minutes

15 Minutes

INGREDIENTS

- 1 cup quinoa, rinsed
- 2 cups water
- 1 ripe avocado, diced
- 1 cup cherry tomatoes, halved
- 1 can (15 oz) black beans, drained and rinsed
- 1/4 cup red onion, finely chopped
- 1/4 cup cilantro, chopped
- Juice of 1 lime
- 2 tablespoons olive oil
- Salt and pepper, to taste

INSTRUCTIONS

1. In a saucepan, bring the quinoa and water to a boil.
2. Reduce heat to low, cover, and simmer for 15 minutes or until the quinoa is cooked and water is absorbed. Fluff with a fork and let it cool.
3. In a large bowl, combine the cooled quinoa, avocado, cherry tomatoes, black beans, red onion, and cilantro.
4. In a small bowl, whisk together lime juice, olive oil, salt, and pepper.
5. Pour the dressing over the salad and toss to combine.
6. Serve chilled or at room temperature.

Lettuce Wraps with Chicken and Hummus

4

10 Minutes

15 Minutes

INGREDIENTS

- 1 lb boneless, skinless chicken breasts, sliced thinly
- 1 tablespoon olive oil
- Salt and pepper, to taste
- 1 teaspoon garlic powder
- 1 teaspoon paprika
- 8 large lettuce leaves (romaine or butter lettuce)
- 1/2 cup hummus
- 1/2 cup shredded carrots
- 1/4 cup sliced cucumbers
- 1/4 cup sliced red bell peppers

INSTRUCTIONS

1. Heat olive oil in a skillet over medium heat.
2. Season the chicken slices with salt, pepper, garlic powder, and paprika.
3. Cook the chicken in the skillet for 6-8 minutes, turning occasionally, until fully cooked.
4. Remove the chicken from heat and let it cool slightly.
5. To assemble the wraps, spread a tablespoon of hummus on each lettuce leaf.
6. Top with chicken slices, shredded carrots, cucumbers, and bell peppers.
7. Roll up the lettuce leaves and serve immediately.

Lentil and Spinach Soup

6

10 Minutes

30 Minutes

INGREDIENTS

- 1 tablespoon olive oil
- 1 onion, diced
- 2 carrots, diced
- 2 celery stalks, diced
- 3 garlic cloves, minced
- 1 cup dried lentils, rinsed
- 6 cups vegetable broth
- 1 can (14.5 oz) diced tomatoes
- 1 teaspoon cumin
- 1 teaspoon paprika
- 4 cups fresh spinach leaves
- Salt and pepper, to taste

INSTRUCTIONS

1. Heat olive oil in a large pot over medium heat.
2. Add onion, carrots, and celery, and cook until softened, about 5 minutes.
3. Stir in the garlic and cook for 1 minute until fragrant.
4. Add the lentils, vegetable broth, diced tomatoes, cumin, and paprika. Bring to a boil.
5. Reduce heat and simmer for 25-30 minutes, or until the lentils are tender.
6. Stir in the spinach and cook until wilted, about 2 minutes.
7. Season with salt and pepper to taste, and serve hot.

Baked Salmon with Asparagus and Lemon

4

10 Minutes

20 Minutes

INGREDIENTS

- 4 salmon fillets
- 1 bunch asparagus, trimmed
- 2 tablespoons olive oil
- 2 lemons (1 sliced, 1 juiced)
- 2 garlic cloves, minced
- Salt and pepper, to taste
- Fresh dill (optional)

INSTRUCTIONS

1. Preheat your oven to 400°F (200°C).
2. Line a baking sheet with parchment paper. Arrange the salmon fillets and asparagus on the sheet.
3. Drizzle olive oil and lemon juice over the salmon and asparagus.
4. Sprinkle minced garlic, salt, and pepper on top.
5. Place lemon slices on the salmon fillets.
6. Bake for 15-20 minutes, until the salmon is cooked through and flakes easily with a fork.
7. Garnish with fresh dill, if desired, and serve.

Arugula Salad with Walnuts, Pears, and Gorgonzola

 4

 10 Minutes

 /

INGREDIENTS

- 4 cups arugula
- 1 pear, thinly sliced
- 1/4 cup walnuts, toasted
- 1/4 cup crumbled gorgonzola cheese
- 2 tablespoons balsamic vinegar
- 2 tablespoons olive oil
- Salt and pepper, to taste

INSTRUCTIONS

1. In a large bowl, combine the arugula, pear slices, toasted walnuts, and gorgonzola.
2. In a small bowl, whisk together balsamic vinegar, olive oil, salt, and pepper.
3. Drizzle the dressing over the salad and toss to coat.
4. Serve immediately.

Buddha Bowl with Brown Rice, Vegetables, and Tofu

 4

15 Minutes

30 Minutes

INGREDIENTS

- 1 cup brown rice
- 1 block (14 oz) firm tofu, drained and cubed
- 2 tablespoons soy sauce
- 1 tablespoon sesame oil
- 1 tablespoon olive oil
- 1 cup broccoli florets
- 1 cup shredded carrots
- 1 cup red cabbage, shredded
- 1 avocado, sliced
- 2 tablespoons sesame seeds
- 2 green onions, sliced
- 1/4 cup tahini sauce or dressing of your choice

INSTRUCTIONS

1. Cook the brown rice according to package instructions and set aside.
2. In a bowl, toss the tofu cubes with soy sauce and sesame oil.
3. Heat olive oil in a skillet over medium heat and cook the tofu until golden brown on all sides, about 8-10 minutes.
4. Steam or lightly sauté the broccoli until tender.
5. To assemble the bowls, divide the brown rice among 4 bowls.
6. Top each bowl with tofu, broccoli, shredded carrots, red cabbage, and avocado slices.
7. Sprinkle with sesame seeds and green onions.
8. Drizzle with tahini sauce or your favorite dressing, and serve.

Zoodles (Zucchini Noodles) with Basil Pesto

4

10 Minutes

5 Minutes

INGREDIENTS

- 4 medium zucchinis,   halved (optional)
  spiralized
- 1 cup fresh basil leaves
- 1/4 cup pine nuts
- 1/4 cup grated
  Parmesan cheese
- 2 garlic cloves
- 1/4 cup olive oil
- Salt and pepper, to taste
- Cherry tomatoes,

INSTRUCTIONS

1. In a food processor, combine basil leaves, pine nuts,
   Parmesan cheese, and garlic. Pulse until finely chopped.
2. With the processor running, slowly add the olive oil until
   the pesto is smooth. Season with salt and pepper to taste.
3. In a large skillet, lightly sauté the zucchini noodles
   (zoodles) over medium heat for 2-3 minutes until just
   tender.
4. Remove from heat and toss with the basil pesto.
5. Serve immediately, garnished with cherry tomatoes if
   desired.

Grilled Chicken with Kale and Apple Salad

4

15 Minutes

15 Minutes

INGREDIENTS

- 4 boneless, skinless chicken
  breasts
- 2 tablespoons olive oil
- Salt and pepper, to taste
- 1 teaspoon garlic powder
- 1 bunch kale, stems removed
  and chopped
- 1 apple, thinly sliced
- 1/4 cup walnuts, toasted
- 1/4 cup feta cheese, crumbled
- 2 tablespoons lemon juice
- 2 tablespoons olive oil (for
  dressing)
- 1 teaspoon honey

INSTRUCTIONS

1. Preheat your grill or grill
   pan over medium-high
   heat.
2. Brush the chicken breasts
   with olive oil and season
   with salt, pepper, and garlic
   powder.
3. Grill the chicken for 6-7
   minutes per side, until fully
   cooked. Let it rest for a few
   minutes before slicing.
4. In a large bowl, combine
   the chopped kale, apple
   slices, toasted walnuts, and
   feta cheese.
5. In a small bowl, whisk
   together lemon juice, olive
   oil, and honey. Pour over
   the salad and toss to coat.
6. Serve the grilled chicken
   slices on top of the kale
   salad.

Sweet Potato and Spinach Frittata

4

10 Minutes

25 Minutes

INGREDIENTS

- 1 tablespoon olive oil
- 1 small onion, diced
- 1 medium sweet potato, peeled and diced
- 2 cups fresh spinach leaves
- 6 large eggs
- 1/4 cup milk
- Salt and pepper, to taste
- 1/4 cup crumbled feta

cheese (optional)

INSTRUCTIONS

1. Preheat your oven to 350°F (175°C).
2. Heat olive oil in an oven-safe skillet over medium heat.
3. Add the diced onion and sweet potato, cooking until the sweet potato is tender, about 10 minutes.
4. Stir in the spinach and cook until wilted, about 2 minutes.
5. In a bowl, whisk together eggs, milk, salt, and pepper. Pour the egg mixture over the vegetables in the skillet.
6. Cook on the stove for 2-3 minutes, then transfer the skillet to the oven.
7. Bake for 15 minutes, or until the frittata is set.
8. Sprinkle with feta cheese before serving, if desired.

Tuna Salad with Avocado and Sunflower Seeds

2

10 Minutes

/

INGREDIENTS

- 1 can (5 oz) tuna, drained
- 1 ripe avocado, diced
- 1 celery stalk, diced
- 2 tablespoons mayonnaise or Greek yogurt
- 1 tablespoon lemon juice
- Salt and pepper, to taste
- 2 tablespoons sunflower seeds
- Lettuce leaves or whole grain bread for serving

INSTRUCTIONS

1. In a medium bowl, combine the drained tuna, diced avocado, and celery.
2. Add mayonnaise or Greek yogurt, lemon juice, salt, and pepper. Mix well to combine.
3. Stir in the sunflower seeds.
4. Serve the tuna salad on lettuce leaves or whole grain bread.

CHAPTER 3
LIGHT AND BALANCED DINNERS

Fish Fillet with Grilled Vegetables

4

10 Minutes

20 Minutes

INGREDIENTS

- 4 fish fillets (such as cod, tilapia, or salmon)
- 2 tablespoons olive oil
- Salt and pepper, to taste
- 1 lemon, sliced
- 1 zucchini, sliced
- 1 red bell pepper, sliced
- 1 yellow bell pepper, sliced
- 1 red onion, sliced
- 2 tablespoons balsamic vinegar

INSTRUCTIONS

1. Preheat your grill or grill pan to medium-high heat.
2. Brush the fish fillets with 1 tablespoon of olive oil and season with salt and pepper.
3. Grill the fish for 4-5 minutes per side, or until the fish flakes easily with a fork. Remove from the grill and set aside.
4. Toss the zucchini, bell peppers, and onion slices with the remaining olive oil and balsamic vinegar. Season with salt and pepper.
5. Grill the vegetables for 5-7 minutes, turning occasionally, until tender and slightly charred.
6. Serve the fish fillets with the grilled vegetables, garnished with lemon slices.

Chicken and Broccoli Stir-Fry with Brown Rice

4

10 Minutes

20 Minutes

INGREDIENTS

- 1 lb boneless, skinless chicken breasts, sliced thinly
- 2 tablespoons soy sauce
- 1 tablespoon sesame oil
- 2 tablespoons olive oil
- 3 cups broccoli florets
- 1 red bell pepper, sliced
- 2 garlic cloves, minced
- 1-inch piece of ginger, grated
- 1 cup cooked brown rice

INSTRUCTIONS

1. In a bowl, toss the chicken slices with soy sauce and sesame oil.
2. Heat 1 tablespoon of olive oil in a large skillet or wok over medium-high heat.
3. Add the chicken and cook for 5-6 minutes, until browned and cooked through. Remove the chicken from the skillet and set aside.
4. Add the remaining olive oil to the skillet. Add the broccoli and bell pepper, cooking for 3-4 minutes until tender-crisp.
5. Stir in the garlic and ginger, cooking for another minute.
6. Return the chicken to the skillet and stir-fry everything together for 2 minutes.
7. Serve the stir-fry over cooked brown rice.

Stuffed Eggplant with Quinoa and Sun-Dried Tomatoes

 4

 15 Minutes

 40 Minutes

INGREDIENTS

- 2 large eggplants, halved lengthwise
- 1 cup cooked quinoa
- 1/2 cup sun-dried tomatoes, chopped
- 1/4 cup feta cheese, crumbled
- 1/4 cup fresh parsley, chopped
- 2 tablespoons olive oil
- 1 garlic clove, minced
- Salt and pepper, to taste

INSTRUCTIONS

1. Preheat your oven to 375°F (190°C).
2. Scoop out the flesh from the eggplant halves, leaving about 1/2 inch of the shell. Chop the scooped-out flesh and set aside.
3. Place the eggplant halves on a baking sheet and brush with 1 tablespoon of olive oil. Bake for 20 minutes until tender.
4. Meanwhile, heat the remaining olive oil in a skillet over medium heat. Add the garlic and chopped eggplant flesh, cooking for 5 minutes.
5. In a bowl, combine the cooked quinoa, sun-dried tomatoes, cooked eggplant mixture, feta cheese, parsley, salt, and pepper.
6. Stuff the baked eggplant halves with the quinoa mixture and return to the oven for another 15 minutes.
7. Serve warm.

Chicken Curry with Coconut Milk and Spinach

 4

 10 Minutes

 25 Minutes

INGREDIENTS

- 1 lb boneless, skinless chicken thighs, cut into bite-sized pieces
- 2 tablespoons olive oil
- 1 onion, diced
- 2 garlic cloves, minced
- 1 tablespoon curry powder
- 1 teaspoon ground cumin
- 1 teaspoon ground turmeric
- 1 can (14 oz) coconut milk
- 4 cups fresh spinach leaves
- Salt and pepper, to taste
- Cooked rice, for serving

INSTRUCTIONS

1. Heat olive oil in a large pot over medium heat. Add the diced onion and cook until softened, about 5 minutes.
2. Stir in the garlic, curry powder, cumin, and turmeric, cooking for 1 minute until fragrant.
3. Add the chicken pieces to the pot and cook until browned, about 5-7 minutes.
4. Pour in the coconut milk and bring the mixture to a simmer. Cook for 15 minutes until the chicken is fully cooked.
5. Stir in the spinach and cook until wilted, about 2 minutes.
6. Season with salt and pepper, and serve the curry over cooked rice.

Pork Chops with Kale and Sweet Potatoes

4

10 Minutes

25 Minutes

INGREDIENTS

- 4 pork chops
- 2 tablespoons olive oil
- Salt and pepper, to taste
- 2 sweet potatoes, peeled and diced
- 1 bunch kale, stems removed and chopped
- 1 garlic clove, minced
- 1/2 teaspoon paprika

INSTRUCTIONS

1. Preheat your oven to 400°F (200°C).
2. Season the pork chops with salt, pepper, and paprika.
3. Heat 1 tablespoon of olive oil in an oven-safe skillet over medium-high heat. Sear the pork chops for 3-4 minutes per side until browned.
4. Transfer the skillet to the oven and bake the pork chops for 10-12 minutes until cooked through. Remove from the oven and set aside.
5. In the same skillet, add the remaining olive oil and diced sweet potatoes. Cook for 8-10 minutes, stirring occasionally, until the sweet potatoes are tender.
6. Stir in the chopped kale and garlic, cooking until the kale is wilted, about 3 minutes.
7. Serve the pork chops with the kale and sweet potatoes.

Chicken Soup with Vegetables and Ginger

6

15 Minutes

45 Minutes

INGREDIENTS

- 1 lb boneless, skinless chicken breasts
- 2 tablespoons olive oil
- 1 onion, diced
- 2 carrots, diced
- 2 celery stalks, diced
- 2 garlic cloves, minced
- 1-inch piece of ginger, sliced
- 8 cups chicken broth
- 1 zucchini, diced
- 2 cups spinach leaves
- Salt and pepper, to taste

INSTRUCTIONS

1. Heat olive oil in a large pot over medium heat. Add the diced onion, carrots, and celery, cooking until softened, about 5 minutes.
2. Stir in the garlic and ginger, cooking for 1 minute until fragrant.
3. Add the chicken breasts and chicken broth to the pot. Bring to a boil, then reduce heat and simmer for 25 minutes.
4. Remove the chicken breasts from the soup and shred them with two forks.
5. Return the shredded chicken to the pot and add the zucchini. Simmer for another 10 minutes until the zucchini is tender.
6. Stir in the spinach leaves and cook until wilted, about 2 minutes.
7. Season with salt and pepper, and serve hot.

Cabbage Tacos with Shrimp and Guacamole

4

15 Minutes

10 Minutes

INGREDIENTS

- 1 lb shrimp, peeled and deveined
- 2 tablespoons olive oil
- 1 teaspoon chili powder
- 1/2 teaspoon cumin
- Salt and pepper, to taste
- 8 large cabbage leaves
- 1 avocado
- 1 lime, juiced
- 1 small tomato, diced
- 1/4 cup red onion, diced
- Fresh cilantro, for garnish

INSTRUCTIONS

1. In a bowl, toss the shrimp with olive oil, chili powder, cumin, salt, and pepper.
2. Heat a skillet over medium-high heat and cook the shrimp for 3-4 minutes per side until fully cooked. Set aside.
3. In a small bowl, mash the avocado with lime juice, tomato, and red onion to make guacamole. Season with salt.
4. To assemble the tacos, place a spoonful of guacamole on each cabbage leaf and top with shrimp.
5. Garnish with fresh cilantro and serve immediately.

Miso Soup with Tofu and Mushrooms

4

10 Minutes

15 Minutes

INGREDIENTS

- 4 cups water
- 3 tablespoons miso paste
- 1 block (14 oz) firm tofu, cubed
- 1 cup mushrooms, sliced (shiitake or button mushrooms)
- 2 green onions, sliced
- 1 sheet nori, cut into small strips (optional)
- 1 tablespoon soy sauce (optional)

INSTRUCTIONS

1. In a medium pot, bring the water to a gentle simmer over medium heat.
2. Stir in the miso paste until fully dissolved.
3. Add the cubed tofu and sliced mushrooms to the pot. Simmer for 5-7 minutes until the mushrooms are tender.
4. Stir in the green onions and nori strips (if using).
5. Season with soy sauce if desired, and serve hot.

Turkey Meatballs with Tomato Sauce and Vegetables

4

15 Minutes

30 Minutes

INGREDIENTS

- 1 lb ground turkey
- 1/4 cup breadcrumbs
- 1/4 cup grated Parmesan cheese
- 1 egg
- 2 garlic cloves, minced
- 1 teaspoon dried oregano
- Salt and pepper, to taste
- 2 tablespoons olive oil
- 1 onion, diced
- 1 carrot, diced
- 1 zucchini, diced
- 1 can (28 oz) crushed tomatoes
- Fresh basil, for garnish

INSTRUCTIONS

1. In a bowl, combine ground turkey, breadcrumbs, Parmesan cheese, egg, garlic, oregano, salt, and pepper. Mix well and form into small meatballs.
2. Heat olive oil in a large skillet over medium heat. Add the meatballs and cook for 5-7 minutes, turning occasionally, until browned on all sides.
3. Remove the meatballs from the skillet and set aside.
4. In the same skillet, add the diced onion, carrot, and zucchini. Cook until softened, about 5 minutes.
5. Stir in the crushed tomatoes and bring to a simmer. Return the meatballs to the skillet, cover, and simmer for 20 minutes until the meatballs are cooked through.
6. Garnish with fresh basil and serve.

Stuffed Bell Peppers with Brown Rice and Black Beans

4

15 Minutes

35 Minutes

INGREDIENTS

- 4 large bell peppers, tops cut off and seeds removed
- 1 cup cooked brown rice
- 1 can (15 oz) black beans, drained and rinsed
- 1/2 cup corn kernels
- 1/2 cup diced tomatoes
- 1 teaspoon cumin
- 1 teaspoon chili powder
- Salt and pepper, to taste
- 1/4 cup shredded cheese (optional)
- Fresh cilantro, for garnish

INSTRUCTIONS

1. Preheat your oven to 375°F (190°C).
2. In a bowl, mix together cooked brown rice, black beans, corn, diced tomatoes, cumin, chili powder, salt, and pepper.
3. Stuff each bell pepper with the rice and bean mixture and place in a baking dish.
4. Cover the dish with foil and bake for 25 minutes.
5. Remove the foil and sprinkle with shredded cheese if using. Bake for an additional 10 minutes until the cheese is melted and the peppers are tender.
6. Garnish with fresh cilantro and serve.

CHAPTER 4
HEALTHY AND DELICIOUS SNACKS

Nut and Seed Energy Bars

 12 Bars

 10 Minutes

 20 Minutes

INGREDIENTS

- 1 cup rolled oats
- 1/2 cup almonds, chopped
- 1/2 cup sunflower seeds
- 1/4 cup flaxseeds
- 1/4 cup honey or maple syrup
- 1/4 cup peanut butter or almond butter
- 1/2 teaspoon vanilla extract
- 1/4 teaspoon salt
- 1/4 cup dried cranberries or raisins

INSTRUCTIONS

1. Preheat your oven to 325°F (160°C). Line an 8x8-inch baking dish with parchment paper.
2. In a large bowl, mix the oats, almonds, sunflower seeds, and flaxseeds.
3. In a small saucepan over low heat, combine honey or maple syrup, peanut butter, vanilla extract, and salt. Stir until smooth and melted.
4. Pour the wet mixture over the dry ingredients and stir until well combined.
5. Fold in the dried cranberries or raisins.
6. Press the mixture firmly into the prepared baking dish.
7. Bake for 15-20 minutes until the edges are golden brown.
8. Let cool completely before cutting into bars.

Kale Chips with Sea Salt

 4

 10 Minutes

 15 Minutes

INGREDIENTS

- 1 bunch kale, washed and dried
- 1 tablespoon olive oil
- 1/2 teaspoon sea salt

INSTRUCTIONS

1. Preheat your oven to 300°F (150°C).
2. Remove the stems from the kale and tear the leaves into bite-sized pieces.
3. Place the kale in a large bowl, drizzle with olive oil, and sprinkle with sea salt. Toss to coat evenly.
4. Spread the kale in a single layer on a baking sheet.
5. Bake for 10-15 minutes, until the edges are crispy but not burnt.
6. Let cool slightly before serving.

Hummus with Carrots and Cucumbers

4

10 Minutes

/

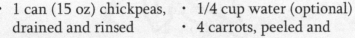

- 1 can (15 oz) chickpeas, drained and rinsed
- 1/4 cup tahini
- 2 tablespoons olive oil
- 2 tablespoons lemon juice
- 1 garlic clove
- 1/2 teaspoon ground cumin
- Salt and pepper, to taste
- 1/4 cup water (optional)
- 4 carrots, peeled and cut into sticks
- 2 cucumbers, sliced

INSTRUCTIONS

1. In a food processor, combine chickpeas, tahini, olive oil, lemon juice, garlic, cumin, salt, and pepper.
2. Blend until smooth, adding water if needed to achieve your desired consistency.
3. Transfer the hummus to a serving bowl.
4. Serve with carrot sticks and cucumber slices.

Greek Yogurt with Dried Fruit

2

5 Minutes

/

INGREDIENTS

- 2 cups Greek yogurt
- 1/4 cup dried fruit (raisins, apricots, cranberries)
- 2 tablespoons honey
- 1/4 cup nuts (optional)

INSTRUCTIONS

1. Divide the Greek yogurt between two bowls.
2. Top each bowl with dried fruit.
3. Drizzle honey over the top.
4. Add nuts if desired, and serve immediately.

Fruit and Vegetable Smoothie

 2

 5 Minutes

/

INGREDIENTS

- 1 banana
- 1/2 cup spinach
- 1/2 cup kale
- 1 apple, cored and chopped
- 1/2 cup frozen berries (strawberries, blueberries, raspberries)
- 1 cup unsweetened almond milk
- 1 tablespoon chia seeds (optional)

INSTRUCTIONS

1. In a blender, combine banana, spinach, kale, apple, frozen berries, and almond milk.
2. Blend until smooth.
3. If using, add chia seeds and blend again for a few seconds.
4. Pour into glasses and serve immediately.

Homemade Popcorn with Coconut Oil

 4

 5 Minutes

10 Minutes

INGREDIENTS

- 1/4 cup popcorn kernels
- 2 tablespoons coconut oil
- 1/2 teaspoon sea salt

INSTRUCTIONS

1. Heat coconut oil in a large pot over medium heat.
2. Add a few popcorn kernels to the pot and cover. Once they pop, add the remaining kernels in an even layer.
3. Cover the pot, and gently shake it to keep the kernels moving as they pop.
4. Once the popping slows to a few seconds between pops, remove the pot from heat.
5. Season with sea salt and toss to coat evenly.
6. Serve immediately.

Trail Mix with Dark Chocolate and Nuts

4

5 Minutes

/

INGREDIENTS

- 1/2 cup almonds
- 1/2 cup walnuts
- 1/4 cup pumpkin seeds
- 1/4 cup dried cranberries
- 1/4 cup dark chocolate chunks or chips

INSTRUCTIONS

1. In a large bowl, combine almonds, walnuts, pumpkin seeds, dried cranberries, and dark chocolate chunks.
2. Mix well.
3. Divide into small portions or store in an airtight container.

Almond Flour Muffins with Blueberries

12 Muffins

10 Minutes

25 Minutes

INGREDIENTS

- 2 cups almond flour
- 1/2 teaspoon baking soda
- 1/4 teaspoon salt
- 3 large eggs
- 1/4 cup honey or maple syrup
- 1/4 cup coconut oil, melted
- 1 teaspoon vanilla extract
- 1 cup fresh or frozen blueberries

INSTRUCTIONS

1. Preheat your oven to 350°F (175°C). Line a muffin tin with paper liners.
2. In a bowl, mix almond flour, baking soda, and salt.
3. In another bowl, whisk together eggs, honey, coconut oil, and vanilla extract.
4. Combine the wet and dry ingredients, mixing until smooth.
5. Fold in the blueberries.
6. Spoon the batter into the muffin tin, filling each cup about 3/4 full.
7. Bake for 20-25 minutes, until a toothpick inserted into the center comes out clean.
8. Let the muffins cool in the tin for a few minutes before transferring to a wire rack.

Guacamole with Sweet Potato Chips

4

15 Minutes

25 Minutes

INGREDIENTS

For the Guacamole:
- 2 ripe avocados
- 1 lime, juiced
- 1 small tomato, diced
- 1/4 cup red onion, diced
- 1 garlic clove, minced
- Salt and pepper, to taste

For the Sweet Potato Chips:
- 2 large sweet potatoes,

sliced thinly
- 2 tablespoons olive oil
- 1/2 teaspoon sea salt
-

INSTRUCTIONS

For the Sweet Potato Chips:
1. Preheat your oven to 375°F (190°C).
2. Toss the sweet potato slices in olive oil and sea salt.
3. Arrange the slices in a single layer on a baking sheet.
4. Bake for 20-25 minutes, flipping halfway, until crisp and golden brown.

For the Guacamole:
1. While the chips are baking, mash the avocados in a bowl.
2. Stir in lime juice, tomato, red onion, garlic, salt, and pepper.
3. Serve the guacamole with the sweet potato chips.

Cucumber Bites with Goat Cheese

4

10 Minutes

/

INGREDIENTS

- 1 large cucumber, sliced into rounds
- 4 oz goat cheese, softened
- 2 tablespoons fresh dill, chopped
- 1 tablespoon olive oil
- Salt and pepper, to taste

INSTRUCTIONS

1. In a small bowl, mix the softened goat cheese with fresh dill, olive oil, salt, and pepper.
2. Spread a small amount of the goat cheese mixture onto each cucumber slice.
3. Arrange on a serving platter and serve immediately.

CHAPTER 5
LOW GLYCEMIC DESSERTS

Almond Flour Brownies with Dark Chocolate

12 Brownies

10 Minutes

25 Minutes

INGREDIENTS

- 1 1/2 cups almond flour
- 1/2 cup unsweetened cocoa powder
- 1/2 teaspoon baking soda
- 1/4 teaspoon salt
- 1/2 cup coconut oil, melted
- 1/2 cup maple syrup or honey
- 2 large eggs
- 1 teaspoon vanilla extract
- 1/2 cup dark chocolate chips

INSTRUCTIONS

1. Preheat your oven to 350°F (175°C). Line an 8x8-inch baking dish with parchment paper.
2. In a bowl, whisk together almond flour, cocoa powder, baking soda, and salt.
3. In another bowl, mix melted coconut oil, maple syrup or honey, eggs, and vanilla extract until smooth.
4. Combine the wet and dry ingredients, mixing until just combined.
5. Fold in the dark chocolate chips.
6. Pour the batter into the prepared baking dish and spread evenly.
7. Bake for 20-25 minutes, or until a toothpick inserted into the center comes out clean.
8. Let the brownies cool completely in the pan before cutting into squares.

Avocado and Cocoa Mousse

4

10 Minutes

30 Minutes

INGREDIENTS

- 2 ripe avocados
- 1/4 cup unsweetened cocoa powder
- 1/4 cup maple syrup or honey
- 1/4 cup almond milk
- 1 teaspoon vanilla extract
- Pinch of salt
- Fresh berries or coconut flakes for garnish (optional)

INSTRUCTIONS

1. In a food processor, blend the avocados, cocoa powder, maple syrup or honey, almond milk, vanilla extract, and salt until smooth and creamy.
2. Taste and adjust sweetness if needed.
3. Spoon the mousse into serving bowls or glasses.
4. Refrigerate for at least 30 minutes before serving.
5. Garnish with fresh berries or coconut flakes, if desired.

Apple and Almond Cake with No Added Sugar

 8

 15 Minutes

 40 Minutes

INGREDIENTS

- 3 large apples, peeled, cored, and grated
- 2 cups almond flour
- 1 teaspoon baking powder
- 1/2 teaspoon ground cinnamon
- 3 large eggs
- 1/4 cup coconut oil, melted
- 1 teaspoon vanilla extract
- 1/2 cup chopped almonds

INSTRUCTIONS

1. Preheat your oven to 350°F (175°C). Grease an 8-inch round cake pan and line the bottom with parchment paper.
2. In a large bowl, mix the grated apples, almond flour, baking powder, cinnamon, eggs, melted coconut oil, and vanilla extract until well combined.
3. Stir in the chopped almonds.
4. Pour the batter into the prepared cake pan and spread evenly.
5. Bake for 35-40 minutes, or until a toothpick inserted into the center comes out clean.
6. Let the cake cool in the pan for 10 minutes before transferring to a wire rack to cool completely.

Lemon Cheesecake with Nut Crust

 8

20 Minutes

45 Minutes

Chilling Time 45 Minutes

INGREDIENTS

For the Crust:
- 1 cup almonds or walnuts, finely ground
- 2 tablespoons coconut oil, melted
- 2 tablespoons honey or maple syrup

For the Filling:
- 16 oz cream cheese, softened
- 1/2 cup Greek yogurt
- 1/4 cup honey or maple syrup
- 2 large eggs
- 1/4 cup fresh lemon juice
- 1 tablespoon lemon zest
- 1 teaspoon vanilla extract

INSTRUCTIONS

1. Preheat your oven to 325°F (160°C). Grease a 9-inch springform pan.
2. In a bowl, mix ground almonds or walnuts, melted coconut oil, and honey or maple syrup until well combined.
3. Press the mixture into the bottom of the prepared pan to form the crust.
4. In a large bowl, beat together cream cheese, Greek yogurt, honey or maple syrup, eggs, lemon juice, lemon zest, and vanilla extract until smooth.
5. Pour the filling over the crust in the pan.
6. Bake for 45 minutes, or until the center is set but still slightly jiggly.
7. Turn off the oven and let the cheesecake cool in the oven with the door slightly open for 1 hour.
8. Refrigerate for at least 4 hours before serving.

Oatmeal and Dark Chocolate Cookies

20 Cookies

10 Minutes

12 Minutes

INGREDIENTS

- 1 1/2 cups rolled oats
- 1/2 cup almond flour
- 1/2 teaspoon baking soda
- 1/4 teaspoon salt
- 1/2 cup coconut oil, melted
- 1/2 cup honey or maple syrup
- 1 large egg
- 1 teaspoon vanilla extract
- 1/2 cup dark chocolate chips

INSTRUCTIONS

1. Preheat your oven to 350°F (175°C). Line a baking sheet with parchment paper.
2. In a bowl, mix together rolled oats, almond flour, baking soda, and salt.
3. In another bowl, whisk together melted coconut oil, honey or maple syrup, egg, and vanilla extract.
4. Combine the wet and dry ingredients, mixing until just combined.
5. Fold in the dark chocolate chips.
6. Drop spoonfuls of dough onto the prepared baking sheet.
7. Bake for 10-12 minutes, or until the edges are golden brown.
8. Let the cookies cool on the baking sheet for a few minutes before transferring to a wire rack to cool completely.

Coconut Milk and Vanilla Panna Cotta

4

10 Minutes

5 Minutes

Chilling Time 45 Minutes

INGREDIENTS

- 1 can (13.5 oz) full-fat coconut milk
- 1/4 cup honey or maple syrup
- 1 teaspoon vanilla extract
- 1 tablespoon gelatin
- 3 tablespoons cold water

INSTRUCTIONS

1. In a small bowl, sprinkle gelatin over cold water and let it sit for 5 minutes to bloom.
2. In a saucepan, heat coconut milk and honey over medium heat until just simmering. Do not boil.
3. Remove from heat and stir in the vanilla extract and bloomed gelatin until fully dissolved.
4. Pour the mixture into individual ramekins or serving glasses.
5. Refrigerate for at least 4 hours, or until set.
6. Serve chilled, with fresh fruit or a drizzle of honey if desired.

Banana and Peanut Butter Ice Cream

 4

 5 Minutes

 2 Hours

INGREDIENTS

- 4 ripe bananas, sliced and frozen
- 1/4 cup peanut butter
- 1 teaspoon vanilla extract
- 1/4 cup almond milk (optional, for a creamier texture)

INSTRUCTIONS

1. Place the frozen banana slices in a food processor and blend until smooth and creamy.
2. Add the peanut butter and vanilla extract, blending until well combined.
3. If the mixture is too thick, add almond milk one tablespoon at a time until the desired consistency is reached.
4. Serve immediately as soft-serve or transfer to a container and freeze for 2 hours for a firmer texture.

Carrot Cake with Greek Yogurt Frosting

 8

 20 Minutes

35 Minutes

INGREDIENTS

For the Cake:
- 1 1/2 cups almond flour
- 1/2 teaspoon baking soda
- 1/2 teaspoon ground cinnamon
- 1/4 teaspoon ground nutmeg
- 1/4 teaspoon salt
- 3 large eggs
- 1/4 cup coconut oil, melted
- 1/4 cup honey or maple syrup
- 1 teaspoon vanilla extract
- 1 1/2 cups grated carrots
- 1/2 cup chopped walnuts or pecans (optional)

For the Frosting:
- 1 cup Greek yogurt
- 2 tablespoons honey or maple syrup
- 1 teaspoon vanilla extract

INSTRUCTIONS

1. Preheat your oven to 350°F (175°C). Grease an 8-inch round cake pan.
2. In a bowl, mix almond flour, baking soda, cinnamon, nutmeg, and salt.
3. In another bowl, whisk together eggs, melted coconut oil, honey or maple syrup, and vanilla extract.
4. Combine the wet and dry ingredients, mixing until smooth.
5. Fold in the grated carrots and chopped nuts, if using.
6. Pour the batter into the prepared cake pan and spread evenly.
7. Bake for 30-35 minutes, or until a toothpick inserted into the center comes out clean.
8. Let the cake cool completely before frosting.
9. For the frosting, mix Greek yogurt, honey, and vanilla extract until smooth. Spread over the cooled cake and serve.

Pumpkin Spice Muffins

12 Muffins

10 Minutes

20 Minutes

INGREDIENTS

- 1 1/2 cups almond flour
- 1/2 cup pumpkin puree
- 1/4 cup honey or maple syrup
- 3 large eggs
- 1/4 cup coconut oil, melted
- 1 teaspoon pumpkin spice
- 1/2 teaspoon baking soda
- 1/4 teaspoon salt

INSTRUCTIONS

1. Preheat your oven to 350°F (175°C). Line a muffin tin with paper liners.
2. In a bowl, whisk together pumpkin puree, honey, eggs, melted coconut oil, and pumpkin spice.
3. Add almond flour, baking soda, and salt to the wet ingredients, mixing until smooth.
4. Spoon the batter into the muffin tin, filling each cup about 3/4 full.
5. Bake for 18-20 minutes, or until a toothpick inserted into the center comes out clean.
6. Let the muffins cool in the tin for a few minutes before transferring to a wire rack.

Berry and Almond Crumble

6

10 Minutes

25 Minutes

INGREDIENTS

For the Filling:
- 4 cups mixed berries (blueberries, raspberries, strawberries)
- 2 tablespoons honey or maple syrup
- 1 tablespoon lemon juice

For the Crumble:
- 1 cup almond flour
- 1/4 cup sliced almonds
- 1/4 cup coconut oil, melted
- 2 tablespoons honey or maple syrup
- 1/2 teaspoon ground cinnamon
- Pinch of salt

INSTRUCTIONS

1. Preheat your oven to 350°F (175°C). Grease a baking dish.
2. In a bowl, mix the berries with honey and lemon juice. Spread the mixture evenly in the baking dish.
3. In another bowl, combine almond flour, sliced almonds, melted coconut oil, honey, cinnamon, and salt to form the crumble topping.
4. Sprinkle the crumble topping over the berry mixture.
5. Bake for 20-25 minutes, or until the topping is golden brown and the berries are bubbling.
6. Let cool slightly before serving.

CHAPTER 6
LOW-CARB RECIPES

Vegetable Frittata with Bacon

 4

10 Minutes

25 Minutes

INGREDIENTS

- 6 large eggs
- 4 slices bacon, chopped
- 1 cup spinach leaves
- 1/2 red bell pepper, diced
- 1/2 zucchini, diced
- 1/4 cup onion, diced
- 1/4 cup shredded cheddar cheese
- Salt and pepper, to taste
- 1 tablespoon olive oil

INSTRUCTIONS

1. Preheat your oven to 375°F (190°C).
2. In a large oven-safe skillet, cook the bacon over medium heat until crispy. Remove the bacon and set aside, leaving the drippings in the skillet.
3. Add olive oil to the skillet if needed, and sauté the onion, bell pepper, and zucchini for about 5 minutes until softened.
4. Add the spinach and cook for another 2 minutes until wilted.
5. In a bowl, whisk the eggs with salt and pepper. Stir in the cooked bacon.
6. Pour the egg mixture over the vegetables in the skillet and cook for 2-3 minutes until the edges start to set.
7. Sprinkle the shredded cheddar cheese on top.
8. Transfer the skillet to the preheated oven and bake for 15-20 minutes, or until the frittata is fully set and slightly golden on top.
9. Let the frittata cool for a few minutes before slicing and serving.

Baked Chicken with Zucchini and Cherry Tomatoes

 4

 10 Minutes

30 Minutes

INGREDIENTS

- 4 boneless, skinless chicken breasts
- 2 zucchinis, sliced
- 1 pint cherry tomatoes
- 2 tablespoons olive oil
- 2 garlic cloves, minced
- 1 teaspoon Italian seasoning
- Salt and pepper, to taste
- Fresh basil leaves for garnish (optional)

INSTRUCTIONS

1. Preheat your oven to 400°F (200°C).
2. Place the chicken breasts in a baking dish. Drizzle with 1 tablespoon of olive oil and season with Italian seasoning, salt, and pepper.
3. In a bowl, toss the sliced zucchini and cherry tomatoes with the remaining olive oil, minced garlic, salt, and pepper.
4. Arrange the vegetables around the chicken in the baking dish.
5. Bake for 25-30 minutes, or until the chicken is fully cooked and the vegetables are tender.
6. Garnish with fresh basil leaves if desired and serve.

Roasted Cauliflower with Cheese and Herbs

4

INGREDIENTS

10 Minutes

25 Minutes

- 1 large cauliflower head, cut into florets
- 2 tablespoons olive oil
- 1/2 teaspoon garlic powder
- 1/2 teaspoon paprika
- Salt and pepper, to taste
- 1/2 cup shredded Parmesan or cheddar cheese
- 2 tablespoons fresh parsley, chopped

INSTRUCTIONS

1. Preheat your oven to 425°F (220°C).
2. In a large bowl, toss the cauliflower florets with olive oil, garlic powder, paprika, salt, and pepper.
3. Spread the cauliflower evenly on a baking sheet lined with parchment paper.
4. Roast for 20 minutes, stirring halfway through.
5. Sprinkle the shredded cheese over the cauliflower and return to the oven for an additional 5 minutes, or until the cheese is melted and golden.
6. Garnish with fresh parsley and serve hot.

Zucchini Noodles with Fresh Tomato Sauce

4

INGREDIENTS

INSTRUCTIONS

15 Minutes

10 Minutes

- 4 medium zucchinis, spiralized into noodles
- 2 tablespoons olive oil
- 3 garlic cloves, minced
- 4 large tomatoes, chopped
- 1/4 cup fresh basil leaves, chopped
- Salt and pepper, to taste
- Grated Parmesan cheese for serving (optional)

1. Heat olive oil in a large skillet over medium heat. Add minced garlic and sauté for 1 minute until fragrant.
2. Add the chopped tomatoes and cook for 5-7 minutes until they break down into a sauce. Season with salt and pepper.
3. Stir in the fresh basil and cook for another minute.
4. Add the zucchini noodles to the skillet and toss to coat with the sauce. Cook for 2-3 minutes until the noodles are tender but not mushy.
5. Serve immediately, topped with grated Parmesan cheese if desired.

Chicken Salad with Avocado and Walnuts

 4

 15 Minutes

 /

INGREDIENTS

- 2 cups cooked chicken, shredded or chopped
- 1 ripe avocado, diced
- 1/2 cup walnuts, chopped
- 1/4 cup red onion, finely chopped
- 1/4 cup celery, diced
- 2 tablespoons mayonnaise or Greek yogurt
- 1 tablespoon lemon juice
- Salt and pepper, to taste
- Mixed greens for serving

INSTRUCTIONS

1. In a large bowl, combine the cooked chicken, diced avocado, chopped walnuts, red onion, and celery.
2. In a small bowl, mix together the mayonnaise or Greek yogurt, lemon juice, salt, and pepper.
3. Pour the dressing over the chicken mixture and toss gently to combine.
4. Serve the chicken salad over a bed of mixed greens.

Turkey Burger with Lettuce and Tomato

 4

 10 Minutes

10 Minutes

INGREDIENTS

- 1 lb ground turkey
- 1/4 cup breadcrumbs
- 1 egg
- 1 garlic clove, minced
- 1 teaspoon Dijon mustard
- 1/2 teaspoon onion powder
- Salt and pepper, to taste
- 4 lettuce leaves
- 1 tomato, sliced
- 4 whole wheat burger buns (optional)
- Condiments of choice (ketchup, mustard, mayo)

INSTRUCTIONS

1. In a bowl, mix together ground turkey, breadcrumbs, egg, minced garlic, Dijon mustard, onion powder, salt, and pepper.
2. Form the mixture into 4 patties.
3. Heat a skillet or grill over medium-high heat and cook the patties for 4-5 minutes per side, until fully cooked through.
4. Assemble the burgers by placing each turkey patty on a lettuce leaf or a whole wheat bun, topped with tomato slices and your favorite condiments.
5. Serve immediately.

Pork Tenderloin with Roasted Cauliflower

 4

10 Minutes

30 Minutes

INGREDIENTS

- 1 pork tenderloin (about 1 lb)
- 1 tablespoon olive oil
- 1 teaspoon garlic powder
- 1 teaspoon paprika
- Salt and pepper, to taste
- 1 large cauliflower head, cut into florets
- 2 tablespoons olive oil

- (for cauliflower)
- 1/2 teaspoon thyme (optional)

INSTRUCTIONS

1. Preheat your oven to 400°F (200°C).
2. Rub the pork tenderloin with olive oil, garlic powder, paprika, salt, and pepper.
3. Place the pork on a baking sheet lined with parchment paper.
4. In a bowl, toss the cauliflower florets with olive oil, salt, pepper, and thyme (if using).
5. Spread the cauliflower around the pork tenderloin on the baking sheet.
6. Roast in the oven for 25-30 minutes, or until the pork reaches an internal temperature of 145°F (63°C) and the cauliflower is golden and tender.
7. Let the pork rest for 5 minutes before slicing and serving with the roasted cauliflower.

Broccoli and Cheese Soup

 4

 10 Minutes

 20 Minutes

INGREDIENTS

- 4 cups broccoli florets
- 1 tablespoon olive oil
- 1 onion, chopped
- 2 garlic cloves, minced
- 4 cups chicken or vegetable broth
- 1 cup shredded cheddar cheese
- 1/2 cup milk or cream
- Salt and pepper, to taste

INSTRUCTIONS

1. Heat olive oil in a large pot over medium heat. Add the chopped onion and garlic, cooking until softened, about 5 minutes.
2. Add the broccoli florets and broth to the pot. Bring to a boil, then reduce heat and simmer for 10-15 minutes until the broccoli is tender.
3. Using an immersion blender, blend the soup until smooth. Alternatively, you can transfer the soup in batches to a blender.
4. Stir in the shredded cheddar cheese and milk or cream. Continue to cook for another 2-3 minutes until the cheese is melted and the soup is creamy.
5. Season with salt and pepper to taste, and serve hot.

Tuna Salad with Hard-Boiled Eggs and Olives

 4

 10 Minutes

 /

INGREDIENTS

- 2 cans (5 oz each) tuna, drained
- 2 hard-boiled eggs, chopped
- 1/4 cup black olives, sliced
- 1/4 cup celery, diced
- 1/4 cup red onion, finely chopped
- 2 tablespoons

- mayonnaise or Greek yogurt
- 1 tablespoon lemon juice
- Salt and pepper, to taste
- Lettuce leaves or whole grain bread for serving

INSTRUCTIONS

1. In a large bowl, combine the drained tuna, chopped hard-boiled eggs, sliced olives, celery, and red onion.
2. In a small bowl, mix together the mayonnaise or Greek yogurt, lemon juice, salt, and pepper.
3. Pour the dressing over the tuna mixture and stir gently to combine.
4. Serve the tuna salad on lettuce leaves or whole grain bread.

Chicken Fajitas with Peppers and Onions

 4

10 Minutes

15 Minutes

INGREDIENTS

- 1 lb boneless, skinless chicken breasts, sliced thinly
- 1 red bell pepper, sliced
- 1 green bell pepper, sliced
- 1 onion, sliced
- 2 tablespoons olive oil
- 1 teaspoon chili powder
- 1/2 teaspoon cumin
- 1/2 teaspoon paprika
- Salt and pepper, to taste
- 8 small tortillas
- Optional toppings: sour cream, salsa, guacamole, shredded cheese

INSTRUCTIONS

1. In a large skillet, heat olive oil over medium-high heat.
2. Add the sliced chicken and cook for 5-7 minutes until browned and cooked through.
3. Remove the chicken from the skillet and set aside.
4. In the same skillet, add the sliced bell peppers and onions. Cook for 5-7 minutes until softened and slightly charred.
5. Return the chicken to the skillet, adding chili powder, cumin, paprika, salt, and pepper. Stir to coat the chicken and vegetables evenly with the spices.
6. Serve the fajita mixture on tortillas with your choice of toppings.

Chickpea and Spinach Curry

4

10 Minutes

20 Minutes

INGREDIENTS

- 1 tablespoon olive oil
- 1 onion, diced
- 2 garlic cloves, minced
- 1 tablespoon ginger, grated
- 1 tablespoon curry powder
- 1 teaspoon ground cumin
- 1 teaspoon ground turmeric
- 1 can (14.5 oz) diced tomatoes
- 1 can (15 oz) chickpeas, drained and rinsed
- 1 can (14 oz) coconut milk
- 4 cups fresh spinach
- Salt and pepper, to taste
- Cooked rice or naan for serving

INSTRUCTIONS

1. Heat olive oil in a large pan over medium heat. Add the diced onion and sauté for 5 minutes until softened.
2. Stir in the garlic, ginger, curry powder, cumin, and turmeric. Cook for 1 minute until fragrant.
3. Add the diced tomatoes and chickpeas. Cook for 5 minutes, allowing the flavors to meld.
4. Pour in the coconut milk and bring the mixture to a simmer. Cook for 10 minutes until the sauce thickens slightly.
5. Stir in the fresh spinach and cook until wilted, about 2 minutes.
6. Season with salt and pepper to taste. Serve over cooked rice or with naan.

Lentil Meatballs with Tomato Sauce

4

20 Minutes

30 Minutes

INGREDIENTS

For the Meatballs:
- 1 cup cooked lentils
- 1/2 cup breadcrumbs
- 1/4 cup grated Parmesan cheese
- 1 egg
- 2 garlic cloves, minced
- 1 teaspoon dried oregano
- Salt and pepper, to taste
- 2 tablespoons olive oil

For the Tomato Sauce:
- 1 tablespoon olive oil
- 1 onion, diced
- 2 garlic cloves, minced
- 1 can (28 oz) crushed tomatoes
- 1 teaspoon dried basil
- 1 teaspoon dried oregano
- Salt and pepper, to taste

INSTRUCTIONS

1. Preheat your oven to 375°F (190°C).
2. In a large bowl, combine cooked lentils, breadcrumbs, Parmesan cheese, egg, minced garlic, oregano, salt, and pepper. Mix well.
3. Form the mixture into small meatballs and place on a baking sheet lined with parchment paper.
4. Drizzle the meatballs with olive oil and bake for 20 minutes until golden brown.
5. While the meatballs are baking, heat olive oil in a large saucepan over medium heat. Add the onion and garlic, cooking until softened, about 5 minutes.
6. Add the crushed tomatoes, basil, oregano, salt, and pepper. Simmer for 15 minutes, stirring occasionally.
7. Add the baked lentil meatballs to the tomato sauce and simmer for an additional 5 minutes.
8. Serve the lentil meatballs with tomato sauce over pasta or with crusty bread.

Stir-Fried Tofu with Mixed Vegetables

 4

 10 Minutes

 15 Minutes

INGREDIENTS

- 1 block (14 oz) firm tofu, drained and cubed
- 2 tablespoons soy sauce
- 1 tablespoon sesame oil
- 2 tablespoons vegetable oil
- 1 red bell pepper, sliced
- 1 yellow bell pepper, sliced
- 1 zucchini, sliced
- 1 carrot, julienned
- 1 cup broccoli florets
- 2 garlic cloves, minced
- 1 tablespoon ginger, grated
- 1 tablespoon cornstarch mixed with 1/4 cup water (optional, for thickening)

INSTRUCTIONS

1. In a bowl, toss the tofu cubes with soy sauce and sesame oil. Set aside to marinate for a few minutes.
2. Heat vegetable oil in a large skillet or wok over medium-high heat.
3. Add the marinated tofu and stir-fry for 5-7 minutes until golden brown. Remove the tofu from the skillet and set aside.
4. In the same skillet, add the garlic and ginger, cooking for 1 minute until fragrant.
5. Add the bell peppers, zucchini, carrot, and broccoli. Stir-fry for 5-7 minutes until the vegetables are tender-crisp.
6. Return the tofu to the skillet and toss to combine. If using, stir in the cornstarch mixture to thicken the sauce.
7. Serve the stir-fried tofu and vegetables over rice or noodles.

Farro Salad with Sun-Dried Tomatoes and Olives

 4

10 Minutes

 25 Minutes

INGREDIENTS

- 3 cups water or vegetable broth
- 1/2 cup sun-dried tomatoes, chopped
- 1/2 cup Kalamata olives, pitted and sliced
- 1/4 cup red onion, finely chopped
- 1/4 cup fresh parsley, chopped
- 2 tablespoons olive oil
- 1 tablespoon balsamic vinegar
- Salt and pepper, to taste

INSTRUCTIONS

1. In a medium pot, bring the farro and water or vegetable broth to a boil. Reduce heat to low, cover, and simmer for 20-25 minutes until the farro is tender. Drain any excess liquid.
2. In a large bowl, combine the cooked farro, sun-dried tomatoes, olives, red onion, and parsley.
3. In a small bowl, whisk together olive oil, balsamic vinegar, salt, and pepper.
4. Pour the dressing over the farro salad and toss to coat.
5. Serve the salad warm or at room temperature.

Black Bean and Corn Soup

4

10 Minutes

20 Minutes

INGREDIENTS

- 1 tablespoon olive oil
- 1 onion, diced
- 2 garlic cloves, minced
- 1 teaspoon ground cumin
- 1 teaspoon chili powder
- 4 cups vegetable broth
- 2 cans (15 oz each) black beans, drained and rinsed
- 1 can (15 oz) corn kernels, drained
- 1 can (14.5 oz) diced tomatoes
- Salt and pepper, to taste
- Fresh cilantro, for garnish

INSTRUCTIONS

1. Heat olive oil in a large pot over medium heat. Add the onion and cook for 5 minutes until softened.
2. Stir in the garlic, cumin, and chili powder, cooking for 1 minute until fragrant.
3. Add the vegetable broth, black beans, corn, and diced tomatoes. Bring to a boil, then reduce heat and simmer for 15 minutes.
4. Season with salt and pepper to taste.
5. Garnish with fresh cilantro and serve hot.

Bean and Quinoa Burgers

4

15 Minutes

15 Minutes

INGREDIENTS

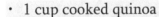

- 1 cup cooked quinoa
- 1 can (15 oz) black beans, drained and rinsed
- 1/4 cup breadcrumbs
- 1/4 cup red onion, finely chopped
- 1 garlic clove, minced
- 1 teaspoon ground cumin
- 1/2 teaspoon paprika
- Salt and pepper, to taste
- 2 tablespoons olive oil
- 4 whole wheat burger buns
- Lettuce, tomato, and condiments for serving

INSTRUCTIONS

1. In a large bowl, mash the black beans with a fork or potato masher.
2. Stir in the cooked quinoa, breadcrumbs, red onion, garlic, cumin, paprika, salt, and pepper. Mix until well combined.
3. Form the mixture into 4 patties.
4. Heat olive oil in a skillet over medium heat. Cook the patties for 5-7 minutes per side until browned and heated through.
5. Serve the bean and quinoa burgers on whole wheat buns with lettuce, tomato, and your favorite condiments.

Stuffed Sweet Potatoes with Avocado and Beans

 4

 10 Minutes

 45 Minutes

INGREDIENTS

- 4 large sweet potatoes
- 1 can (15 oz) black beans, drained and rinsed
- 1 avocado, diced
- 1/2 cup corn kernels
- 1/4 cup red onion, diced
- 1 tablespoon lime juice
- 1 teaspoon ground cumin
- Salt and pepper, to taste
- Fresh cilantro, for garnish

INSTRUCTIONS

1. Preheat your oven to 400°F (200°C).
2. Pierce the sweet potatoes with a fork and place them on a baking sheet. Bake for 40-45 minutes, or until tender.
3. While the sweet potatoes are baking, combine the black beans, avocado, corn, red onion, lime juice, cumin, salt, and pepper in a bowl.
4. Once the sweet potatoes are cooked, let them cool slightly before slicing them open.
5. Stuff each sweet potato with the avocado and bean mixture.
6. Garnish with fresh cilantro and serve.

Tomato and Basil Soup

 4

10 Minutes

20 Minutes

INGREDIENTS

- 2 tablespoons olive oil
- 1 onion, diced
- 3 garlic cloves, minced
- 4 cups fresh tomatoes, chopped (or 2 cans (14.5 oz) diced tomatoes)
- 2 cups vegetable broth
- 1/2 cup fresh basil leaves, chopped
- Salt and pepper, to taste
- 1/4 cup heavy cream or coconut milk (optional)

INSTRUCTIONS

1. Heat olive oil in a large pot over medium heat. Add the onion and cook for 5 minutes until softened.
2. Stir in the garlic and cook for 1 minute until fragrant.
3. Add the chopped tomatoes and vegetable broth. Bring to a boil, then reduce heat and simmer for 15 minutes.
4. Use an immersion blender to blend the soup until smooth. Alternatively, you can transfer the soup in batches to a blender.
5. Stir in the fresh basil, and season with salt and pepper to taste.
6. If using, add the heavy cream or coconut milk and heat through.
7. Serve hot with crusty bread.

Cauliflower Risotto with Mushrooms

4

10 Minutes

25 Minutes

INGREDIENTS

- 1 large cauliflower, grated or riced
- 2 tablespoons olive oil
- 1 onion, diced
- 2 garlic cloves, minced
- 8 oz mushrooms, sliced
- 1/4 cup vegetable broth
- 1/4 cup grated Parmesan cheese
- 1/4 cup chopped parsley
- Salt and pepper, to taste

INSTRUCTIONS

1. Heat olive oil in a large skillet over medium heat. Add the onion and cook for 5 minutes until softened.
2. Stir in the garlic and cook for 1 minute.
3. Add the mushrooms and cook for 5-7 minutes until they release their moisture and are golden brown.
4. Stir in the grated cauliflower and vegetable broth. Cook for 10 minutes until the cauliflower is tender and the liquid is absorbed.
5. Stir in the Parmesan cheese and chopped parsley. Season with salt and pepper to taste.
6. Serve hot.

Zucchini Noodles with Walnut Pesto

4

15 Minutes

5 Minutes

INGREDIENTS

- 4 medium zucchinis, spiralized into noodles
- 1 cup fresh basil leaves
- 1/2 cup walnuts
- 1/4 cup grated Parmesan cheese
- 2 garlic cloves
- 1/4 cup olive oil
- Salt and pepper, to taste
- Cherry tomatoes for garnish (optional)

INSTRUCTIONS

1. In a food processor, combine basil leaves, walnuts, Parmesan cheese, and garlic. Pulse until finely chopped.
2. With the processor running, slowly add the olive oil until the pesto is smooth. Season with salt and pepper to taste.
3. Lightly sauté the zucchini noodles in a large skillet over medium heat for 2-3 minutes until just tender.
4. Toss the noodles with the walnut pesto.
5. Serve immediately, garnished with cherry tomatoes if desired.

CHAPTER 8
SIDE DISHES AND SAUCES

Guacamole with Lime and Cilantro

 4

 10 Minutes

 /

INGREDIENTS

- 3 ripe avocados
- 1 lime, juiced
- 1/4 cup fresh cilantro, chopped
- 1/4 cup red onion, finely diced
- 1 garlic clove, minced
- Salt and pepper, to taste
- 1 small tomato, diced   (optional)

INSTRUCTIONS

1. Cut the avocados in half, remove the pit, and scoop the flesh into a bowl.
2. Mash the avocado with a fork until smooth, leaving some chunks for texture.
3. Stir in the lime juice, cilantro, red onion, minced garlic, salt, and pepper.
4. If using, gently fold in the diced tomato.
5. Taste and adjust seasoning if needed.
6. Serve immediately with tortilla chips or as a topping for tacos.

Beet Hummus

 4

15 Minutes

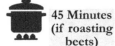 45 Minutes (if roasting beets)

INGREDIENTS

- 1 medium beet, roasted and peeled
- 1 can (15 oz) chickpeas, drained and rinsed
- 2 tablespoons tahini
- 2 tablespoons olive oil
- 2 tablespoons lemon juice
- 1 garlic clove
- Salt and pepper, to taste
- 1/4 cup water (optional, for consistency)

INSTRUCTIONS

1. If you haven't roasted the beet yet, preheat your oven to 400°F (200°C), wrap the beet in foil, and roast for 45 minutes or until tender. Let it cool and peel.
2. In a food processor, combine the roasted beet, chickpeas, tahini, olive oil, lemon juice, garlic, salt, and pepper.
3. Blend until smooth, adding water if needed to reach your desired consistency.
4. Taste and adjust seasoning as needed.
5. Serve with pita chips or fresh vegetables.

Roasted Sweet Potatoes with Rosemary

 4

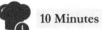 10 Minutes

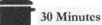 30 Minutes

INGREDIENTS

- 4 medium sweet potatoes, peeled and cubed
- 2 tablespoons olive oil
- 2 teaspoons fresh rosemary, chopped
- Salt and pepper, to taste

INSTRUCTIONS

1. Preheat your oven to 425°F (220°C).
2. In a large bowl, toss the sweet potato cubes with olive oil, rosemary, salt, and pepper.
3. Spread the sweet potatoes in a single layer on a baking sheet.
4. Roast for 25-30 minutes, turning once halfway through, until the sweet potatoes are tender and golden brown.
5. Serve hot as a side dish.

Brussels Sprouts with Walnuts and Honey

4

 10 Minutes

 20 Minutes

INGREDIENTS

- 1 lb Brussels sprouts, trimmed and halved
- 2 tablespoons olive oil
- 1/4 cup walnuts, chopped
- 2 tablespoons honey
- Salt and pepper, to taste

INSTRUCTIONS

1. Preheat your oven to 400°F (200°C).
2. Toss the Brussels sprouts with olive oil, salt, and pepper in a bowl.
3. Spread them out on a baking sheet in a single layer.
4. Roast for 15 minutes, then add the chopped walnuts and roast for an additional 5 minutes until the Brussels sprouts are tender and caramelized.
5. Drizzle with honey and toss to coat before serving.

Cucumber Salad with Dill and Yogurt

 4

 10 Minutes

 /

INGREDIENTS

- 2 large cucumbers, thinly sliced
- 1 cup Greek yogurt
- 2 tablespoons fresh dill, chopped
- 1 tablespoon lemon juice
- 1 garlic clove, minced
- Salt and pepper, to taste

INSTRUCTIONS

1. In a large bowl, combine the sliced cucumbers, Greek yogurt, dill, lemon juice, minced garlic, salt, and pepper.
2. Toss until the cucumbers are well coated with the yogurt mixture.
3. Serve immediately or refrigerate for up to 1 hour before serving to allow the flavors to meld.

Tzatziki Sauce with Cucumbers and Garlic

 4

 10 Minutes

30 Minutes

INGREDIENTS

- 1 cup Greek yogurt
- 1/2 cucumber, grated and drained
- 2 garlic cloves, minced
- 1 tablespoon olive oil
- 1 tablespoon lemon juice
- 1 tablespoon fresh dill, chopped
- Salt and pepper, to taste

INSTRUCTIONS

1. Grate the cucumber and place it in a fine mesh strainer. Press out as much liquid as possible.
2. In a bowl, mix the Greek yogurt, grated cucumber, minced garlic, olive oil, lemon juice, dill, salt, and pepper.
3. Stir until well combined.
4. Cover and refrigerate for at least 30 minutes to let the flavors develop.
5. Serve as a dip or sauce with grilled meats or vegetables.

Fresh Tomato Sauce

INGREDIENTS

10 Minutes

30 Minutes

4

- 4 large tomatoes, chopped
- 2 tablespoons olive oil
- 1 onion, finely chopped
- 3 garlic cloves, minced
- 1/4 cup fresh basil leaves, chopped
- Salt and pepper, to taste
- 1 teaspoon sugar (optional)

INSTRUCTIONS

1. Heat olive oil in a large skillet over medium heat. Add the onion and cook for 5 minutes until softened.
2. Stir in the garlic and cook for 1 minute until fragrant.
3. Add the chopped tomatoes and bring to a simmer.
4. Cook the sauce for 20-25 minutes until it thickens, stirring occasionally.
5. Stir in the fresh basil and season with salt, pepper, and sugar (if using) to taste.
6. Serve over pasta, pizza, or as a base for other dishes.

Brown Rice with Lime and Cilantro

4

INGREDIENTS

5 Minutes

45 Minutes

- 1 cup brown rice
- 2 cups water or vegetable broth
- 1 tablespoon olive oil
- 1 lime, juiced and zested
- 1/4 cup fresh cilantro, chopped
- Salt, to taste

INSTRUCTIONS

1. In a medium saucepan, bring the water or vegetable broth to a boil. Add the brown rice and olive oil.
2. Reduce the heat to low, cover, and simmer for 40-45 minutes until the rice is tender and the liquid is absorbed.
3. Fluff the rice with a fork and stir in the lime juice, lime zest, and chopped cilantro.
4. Season with salt to taste and serve as a side dish.

Grilled Eggplant with Parsley and Garlic

 4

 10 Minutes

15 Minutes

INGREDIENTS

- 2 large eggplants, sliced into rounds
- 3 tablespoons olive oil
- 2 garlic cloves, minced
- 1/4 cup fresh parsley, chopped
- Salt and pepper, to taste

INSTRUCTIONS

1. Preheat your grill or grill pan to medium-high heat.
2. Brush the eggplant slices with olive oil and season with salt and pepper.
3. Grill the eggplant for 5-7 minutes per side until tender and grill marks appear.
4. In a small bowl, mix the minced garlic and chopped parsley.
5. Once the eggplant is done, transfer to a serving plate and sprinkle with the garlic and parsley mixture.
6. Serve hot as a side dish or appetizer.

New Potatoes with Fresh Herbs

 4

 10 Minutes

20 Minutes

INGREDIENTS

- 1 lb new potatoes, halved
- 2 tablespoons olive oil
- 2 tablespoons fresh herbs (such as parsley, dill, or chives), chopped
- Salt and pepper, to taste

INSTRUCTIONS

1. Place the new potatoes in a large pot and cover with water. Add a pinch of salt.
2. Bring to a boil over high heat, then reduce the heat and simmer for 15-20 minutes until the potatoes are tender.
3. Drain the potatoes and return them to the pot.
4. Drizzle with olive oil and toss with the fresh herbs, salt, and pepper.
5. Serve warm as a side dish.

CHAPTER 9
MAKE-AHEAD MEALS

Marinated Chicken with Vegetables

4

15 Minutes
(plus 30
minutes
marinating
time)

INGREDIENTS

- 4 boneless, skinless chicken breasts
- 1/4 cup olive oil
- 2 tablespoons lemon juice
- 2 garlic cloves, minced
- 1 teaspoon dried oregano
- Salt and pepper, to taste

- 2 zucchinis, sliced
- 1 red bell pepper, sliced
- 1 yellow bell pepper, sliced
- 1 red onion, sliced

INSTRUCTIONS

1. In a bowl, mix olive oil, lemon juice, minced garlic, oregano, salt, and pepper to make the marinade.
2. Place the chicken breasts in a resealable plastic bag or shallow dish and pour the marinade over them. Marinate for at least 30 minutes in the refrigerator.
3. Preheat your grill or grill pan to medium-high heat.
4. Grill the chicken for 6-7 minutes per side, or until fully cooked. Set aside.
5. In the same grill or a separate grill pan, cook the sliced vegetables for about 5-7 minutes, until tender and slightly charred.
6. Serve the grilled chicken with the vegetables on the side.

Vegetable and Lentil Soup

6

10 Minutes

40 Minutes

INGREDIENTS

- 1 tablespoon olive oil
- 1 onion, diced
- 2 carrots, diced
- 2 celery stalks, diced
- 3 garlic cloves, minced
- 1 cup dried lentils, rinsed
- 6 cups vegetable broth
- 1 can (14.5 oz) diced tomatoes
- 1 zucchini, diced
- 1 teaspoon dried thyme
- 1 teaspoon dried basil
- Salt and pepper, to taste
- 2 cups spinach leaves

INSTRUCTIONS

1. Heat olive oil in a large pot over medium heat. Add the onion, carrots, and celery, and cook for 5 minutes until softened.
2. Stir in the garlic and cook for 1 minute until fragrant.
3. Add the lentils, vegetable broth, diced tomatoes, zucchini, thyme, basil, salt, and pepper. Bring to a boil.
4. Reduce the heat and simmer for 30 minutes until the lentils are tender.
5. Stir in the spinach leaves and cook for another 2-3 minutes until wilted.
6. Serve hot with crusty bread.

Black Bean and Tomato Chili

 4

 10 Minutes

 30 Minutes

INGREDIENTS

- 1 tablespoon olive oil
- 1 onion, diced
- 3 garlic cloves, minced
- 1 red bell pepper, diced
- 1 green bell pepper, diced
- 1 tablespoon chili powder
- 1 teaspoon ground cumin
- 1 teaspoon smoked paprika
- 1 can (15 oz) black beans, drained and rinsed
- 1 can (14.5 oz) diced tomatoes
- 1 cup vegetable broth
- Salt and pepper, to taste
- 1/4 cup fresh cilantro, chopped

INSTRUCTIONS

1. Heat olive oil in a large pot over medium heat. Add the onion and garlic, and cook for 3-4 minutes until softened.
2. Add the bell peppers and cook for another 5 minutes.
3. Stir in the chili powder, cumin, and smoked paprika, and cook for 1 minute until fragrant.
4. Add the black beans, diced tomatoes, and vegetable broth. Bring to a simmer.
5. Cook for 20 minutes, stirring occasionally, until the chili thickens.
6. Season with salt and pepper, and stir in the chopped cilantro before serving.

Zucchini and Meat Lasagna

 6

 20 Minutes

45 Minutes

INGREDIENTS

- 2 large zucchinis, sliced lengthwise into thin strips
- 1 lb ground beef or turkey
- 1 onion, diced
- 3 garlic cloves, minced
- 1 can (15 oz) tomato sauce
- 1 teaspoon dried oregano
- 1 teaspoon dried basil
- Salt and pepper, to taste
- 1 cup ricotta cheese
- 1 cup shredded mozzarella cheese
- 1/4 cup grated Parmesan cheese

INSTRUCTIONS

1. Preheat your oven to 375°F (190°C).
2. In a large skillet, cook the ground beef or turkey over medium heat until browned. Drain excess fat.
3. Add the onion and garlic, cooking for 3-4 minutes until softened.
4. Stir in the tomato sauce, oregano, basil, salt, and pepper. Simmer for 10 minutes.
5. In a 9x13-inch baking dish, spread a layer of meat sauce.
6. Add a layer of zucchini slices over the sauce.
7. Spread a layer of ricotta cheese over the zucchini, followed by a layer of mozzarella.
8. Repeat the layers, ending with a final layer of meat sauce and a sprinkle of Parmesan cheese on top.
9. Cover with foil and bake for 30 minutes. Remove the foil and bake for an additional 15 minutes until the cheese is bubbly and golden.
10. Let the lasagna rest for 10 minutes before slicing and serving.

Turkey Meatballs with Tomato Sauce

4

15 Minutes

30 Minutes

INGREDIENTS

- 1 lb ground turkey
- 1/4 cup breadcrumbs
- 1/4 cup grated Parmesan cheese
- 1 egg
- 2 garlic cloves, minced
- 1 teaspoon dried oregano
- Salt and pepper, to taste
- 2 tablespoons olive oil
- 1 can (28 oz) crushed tomatoes
- 1/2 teaspoon red pepper flakes (optional)
- Fresh basil for garnish

INSTRUCTIONS

1. Preheat your oven to 375°F (190°C).
2. In a bowl, mix together the ground turkey, breadcrumbs, Parmesan cheese, egg, minced garlic, oregano, salt, and pepper.
3. Form the mixture into small meatballs and place them on a baking sheet lined with parchment paper.
4. Bake the meatballs for 20-25 minutes, or until firm and lightly browned.
5. While the meatballs are baking, heat olive oil in a saucepan over medium heat. Add the crushed tomatoes and red pepper flakes, and simmer for 10-15 minutes until slightly thickened.
6. Once the meatballs are done, add them to the tomato sauce and cook for another 5 minutes.
7. Serve the turkey meatballs with tomato sauce, garnished with fresh basil.

Brown Rice Salad with Vegetables

4

10 Minutes

45 Minutes

INGREDIENTS

- 1 cup brown rice
- 2 cups water or vegetable broth
- 1 red bell pepper, diced
- 1 cucumber, diced
- 1/4 cup red onion, finely chopped
- 1/4 cup fresh parsley, chopped
- 2 tablespoons olive oil
- 1 tablespoon lemon juice
- Salt and pepper, to taste

INSTRUCTIONS

1. In a medium saucepan, bring the water or vegetable broth to a boil. Add the brown rice and olive oil.
2. Reduce the heat to low, cover, and simmer for 40-45 minutes until the rice is tender and the liquid is absorbed.
3. Let the rice cool to room temperature.
4. In a large bowl, combine the cooked rice, diced bell pepper, cucumber, red onion, and parsley.
5. Drizzle with olive oil and lemon juice, and toss to coat.
6. Season with salt and pepper to taste, and serve chilled or at room temperature.

Chicken Cacciatore with Mushrooms

 4

 10 Minutes

 40 Minutes

INGREDIENTS

- 4 boneless, skinless chicken thighs
- 2 tablespoons olive oil
- 1 onion, sliced
- 3 garlic cloves, minced
- 8 oz mushrooms, sliced
- 1 can (14.5 oz) diced tomatoes
- 1/2 cup chicken broth
- 1/2 cup red wine

- (optional)
- 1 teaspoon dried oregano
- 1 teaspoon dried basil
- Salt and pepper, to taste
- Fresh parsley for garnish

INSTRUCTIONS

1. Heat olive oil in a large skillet over medium heat. Add the chicken thighs and cook for 4-5 minutes per side until browned. Remove and set aside.
2. In the same skillet, add the sliced onion and cook for 5 minutes until softened.
3. Stir in the garlic and mushrooms, cooking for another 3-4 minutes.
4. Add the diced tomatoes, chicken broth, red wine (if using), oregano, basil, salt, and pepper. Bring to a simmer.
5. Return the chicken thighs to the skillet and spoon some of the sauce over them.
6. Cover and simmer for 30 minutes until the chicken is fully cooked and the sauce has thickened.
7. Garnish with fresh parsley and serve with pasta, rice, or crusty bread.

Chickpea and Spinach Stew

 4

10 Minutes

25 Minutes

INGREDIENTS

- 2 tablespoons olive oil
- 1 onion, diced
- 3 garlic cloves, minced
- 1 teaspoon ground cumin
- 1/2 teaspoon ground coriander
- 1/2 teaspoon smoked paprika
- 1 can (15 oz) chickpeas, drained and rinsed
- 1 can (14.5 oz) diced tomatoes
- 4 cups fresh spinach leaves
- Salt and pepper, to taste
- 1/4 cup fresh cilantro, chopped

INSTRUCTIONS

1. Heat olive oil in a large pot over medium heat. Add the onion and cook for 5 minutes until softened.
2. Stir in the garlic, cumin, coriander, and smoked paprika. Cook for 1 minute until fragrant.
3. Add the chickpeas and diced tomatoes, and bring to a simmer.
4. Cook for 15 minutes until the flavors meld and the stew thickens.
5. Stir in the spinach and cook until wilted, about 2-3 minutes.
6. Season with salt and pepper, and garnish with fresh cilantro before serving.

Vegetable Curry with Coconut Milk

4

10 Minutes

25 Minutes

INGREDIENTS

- 2 tablespoons olive oil
- 1 onion, diced
- 2 garlic cloves, minced
- 1 tablespoon grated ginger
- 2 tablespoons curry powder
- 1 teaspoon ground cumin
- 1 teaspoon ground turmeric
- 1 can (14 oz) coconut milk
- 2 cups mixed vegetables (such as carrots, bell peppers, and zucchini), chopped
- 1 can (14.5 oz) diced tomatoes
- Salt and pepper, to taste
- 1/4 cup fresh cilantro, chopped

INSTRUCTIONS

1. Heat olive oil in a large pot over medium heat. Add the onion and cook for 5 minutes until softened.
2. Stir in the garlic, ginger, curry powder, cumin, and turmeric. Cook for 1 minute until fragrant.
3. Add the mixed vegetables and cook for 5 minutes until they start to soften.
4. Pour in the coconut milk and diced tomatoes, and bring to a simmer.
5. Cook for 15 minutes until the vegetables are tender and the sauce thickens.
6. Season with salt and pepper, and garnish with fresh cilantro before serving.

Baked Vegetable Frittata

4

10 Minutes

25 Minutes

INGREDIENTS

- 6 large eggs
- 1/4 cup milk or cream
- Salt and pepper, to taste
- 1 tablespoon olive oil
- 1 onion, diced
- 1 zucchini, diced
- 1 red bell pepper, diced
- 1/4 cup shredded cheese (optional)
- Fresh herbs for garnish (such as parsley or chives)

INSTRUCTIONS

1. Preheat your oven to 375°F (190°C).
2. In a large bowl, whisk together the eggs, milk, salt, and pepper.
3. Heat olive oil in an oven-safe skillet over medium heat. Add the onion, zucchini, and red bell pepper, and cook for 5-7 minutes until the vegetables are tender.
4. Pour the egg mixture over the vegetables in the skillet, stirring gently to combine.
5. If using, sprinkle the shredded cheese on top.
6. Transfer the skillet to the oven and bake for 15-20 minutes, or until the frittata is set and slightly golden on top.
7. Let the frittata cool for a few minutes before slicing and garnishing with fresh herbs. Serve warm.

CHAPTER 10
QUICK RECIPES FOR ANY MOMENT

Cucumber and Avocado Salad

 4

10 Minutes

/

INGREDIENTS

- 2 large cucumbers, peeled and diced
- 2 ripe avocados, diced
- 1/4 cup red onion, finely chopped
- 2 tablespoons fresh cilantro, chopped
- 1 tablespoon lime juice
- Salt and pepper, to taste

INSTRUCTIONS

1. In a large bowl, combine the diced cucumbers, avocados, red onion, and cilantro.
2. Drizzle with lime juice and season with salt and pepper.
3. Toss gently to combine, ensuring the avocado stays intact.
4. Serve immediately or refrigerate for up to 30 minutes before serving.

Greek Yogurt with Flaxseeds and Berries

 2

 5 Minutes

 /

INGREDIENTS

- 2 cups Greek yogurt
- 2 tablespoons ground flaxseeds
- 1 cup mixed berries (blueberries, strawberries, raspberries)
- 1 tablespoon honey (optional)

INSTRUCTIONS

1. Divide the Greek yogurt between two bowls.
2. Sprinkle 1 tablespoon of ground flaxseeds over each serving of yogurt.
3. Top each bowl with 1/2 cup of mixed berries.
4. Drizzle with honey if desired, and serve immediately.

Whole Grain Toast with Hummus and Cherry Tomatoes

2

5 Minutes

2 Minutes

INGREDIENTS

- 4 slices whole grain bread
- 1/2 cup hummus
- 1 cup cherry tomatoes, halved
- Salt and pepper, to taste
- Fresh basil leaves for garnish (optional)

INSTRUCTIONS

1. Toast the slices of whole grain bread until golden brown.
2. Spread 2 tablespoons of hummus on each slice of toast.
3. Top with halved cherry tomatoes, and season with salt and pepper.
4. Garnish with fresh basil leaves if desired, and serve immediately.

Matcha Smoothie with Almond Milk

2

5 Minutes

/

INGREDIENTS

- 2 teaspoons matcha powder
- 1 cup unsweetened almond milk
- 1 banana
- 1/2 cup frozen spinach
- 1 tablespoon honey or maple syrup (optional)
- 1/2 cup ice cubes

INSTRUCTIONS

1. In a blender, combine matcha powder, almond milk, banana, frozen spinach, honey or maple syrup (if using), and ice cubes.
2. Blend until smooth and creamy.
3. Pour into glasses and serve immediately.

Fruit Salad with Hemp Seeds

4

10 Minutes

/

INGREDIENTS

- 2 cups mixed fruit (such as berries, melon, pineapple, and grapes)
- 1 tablespoon hemp seeds
- 1 tablespoon fresh mint leaves, chopped (optional)
- 1 tablespoon lime juice

INSTRUCTIONS

1. In a large bowl, combine the mixed fruit.
2. Sprinkle with hemp seeds and chopped mint leaves (if using).
3. Drizzle with lime juice and toss gently to combine.
4. Serve immediately.

Carrot Sticks with Tahini Sauce

4

10 Minutes

/

INGREDIENTS

- 4 large carrots, peeled and cut into sticks
- 1/4 cup tahini
- 2 tablespoons lemon juice
- 1 garlic clove, minced
- 2 tablespoons water (optional, for consistency)
- Salt and pepper, to taste

INSTRUCTIONS

1. In a small bowl, mix the tahini, lemon juice, minced garlic, salt, and pepper. Add water if needed to reach your desired consistency.
2. Arrange the carrot sticks on a serving platter.
3. Serve the tahini sauce alongside the carrot sticks for dipping.

Berry Smoothie with Plant-Based Protein

2

5 Minutes

/

INGREDIENTS

- 1 cup mixed berries (blueberries, strawberries, raspberries)
- 1 scoop plant-based protein powder
- 1 cup unsweetened almond milk
- 1/2 banana
- 1/2 cup ice cubes

INSTRUCTIONS

1. In a blender, combine the mixed berries, plant-based protein powder, almond milk, banana, and ice cubes.
2. Blend until smooth and creamy.
3. Pour into glasses and serve immediately.

Avocado Stuffed with Hard-Boiled Egg

2

10 Minutes

10 Minutes

INGREDIENTS

- 2 ripe avocados, halved and pitted
- 2 hard-boiled eggs, chopped
- 1 tablespoon mayonnaise or Greek yogurt
- 1 teaspoon Dijon mustard
- Salt and pepper, to taste
- Paprika for garnish (optional)

INSTRUCTIONS

1. In a small bowl, mix the chopped hard-boiled eggs with mayonnaise or Greek yogurt, Dijon mustard, salt, and pepper.
2. Spoon the egg mixture into the cavity of each avocado half.
3. Sprinkle with paprika if desired, and serve immediately.

Kale Salad with Apples and Walnuts

 4

 10 Minutes

 /

INGREDIENTS

- 4 cups kale, chopped
- 1 apple, thinly sliced
- 1/4 cup walnuts, chopped
- 2 tablespoons olive oil
- 1 tablespoon lemon juice
- Salt and pepper, to taste

INSTRUCTIONS

1. In a large bowl, combine the chopped kale, apple slices, and chopped walnuts.
2. In a small bowl, whisk together the olive oil, lemon juice, salt, and pepper.
3. Pour the dressing over the salad and toss to coat evenly.
4. Serve immediately.

Pea and Mint Soup

 4

 10 Minutes

 15 Minutes

INGREDIENTS

- 1 tablespoon olive oil
- 1 onion, diced
- 3 cups frozen peas
- 4 cups vegetable broth
- 1/4 cup fresh mint leaves, chopped
- Salt and pepper, to taste
- 1/4 cup Greek yogurt (optional, for garnish)

INSTRUCTIONS

1. Heat olive oil in a large pot over medium heat. Add the diced onion and cook for 5 minutes until softened.
2. Add the frozen peas and vegetable broth. Bring to a boil, then reduce the heat and simmer for 10 minutes.
3. Stir in the fresh mint leaves and cook for another 2 minutes.
4. Use an immersion blender to puree the soup until smooth. Season with salt and pepper.
5. Serve hot, garnished with a dollop of Greek yogurt if desired.

Whole Grain Toast with Almond Butter and Banana

2

5 Minutes

2 Minutes

INGREDIENTS

- 4 slices whole grain bread
- 1/4 cup almond butter
- 1 banana, sliced
- Honey (optional, for drizzling)

INSTRUCTIONS

1. Toast the slices of whole grain bread until golden brown.
2. Spread almond butter on each slice of toast.
3. Top with banana slices and drizzle with honey if desired.
4. Serve immediately.

Endive Boats with Guacamole

4

10 Minutes

/

INGREDIENTS

- 4 endive heads, leaves separated
- 2 ripe avocados
- 1 lime, juiced
- 1/4 cup red onion, finely diced
- 1 garlic clove, minced
- Salt and pepper, to taste
- 1 small tomato, diced (optional)

INSTRUCTIONS

1. In a bowl, mash the avocados with lime juice, red onion, minced garlic, salt, and pepper. Fold in the diced tomato if using.
2. Spoon the guacamole into the endive leaves to create "boats."
3. Arrange the endive boats on a serving platter and serve immediately.

Cacao and Avocado Smoothie

 2

 5 Minutes

 /

INGREDIENTS

- 1 ripe avocado
- 1 tablespoon unsweetened cacao powder
- 1 cup almond milk
- 1 tablespoon honey or maple syrup
- 1/2 cup ice cubes

INSTRUCTIONS

1. In a blender, combine the avocado, cacao powder, almond milk, honey or maple syrup, and ice cubes.
2. Blend until smooth and creamy.
3. Pour into glasses and serve immediately.

Arugula Salad with Strawberries and Almonds

 4

  10 Minutes

/

INGREDIENTS

- 4 cups arugula
- 1 cup strawberries, sliced
- 1/4 cup sliced almonds
- 2 tablespoons balsamic vinegar
- 2 tablespoons olive oil
- Salt and pepper, to taste

INSTRUCTIONS

1. In a large bowl, combine the arugula, sliced strawberries, and sliced almonds.
2. In a small bowl, whisk together the balsamic vinegar, olive oil, salt, and pepper.
3. Drizzle the dressing over the salad and toss to coat evenly.
4. Serve immediately.

Instant Oatmeal with Peanut Butter

2

5 Minutes

2 Minutes

INGREDIENTS

- 1 cup instant oats
- 1 1/2 cups water or milk
- 2 tablespoons peanut butter
- 1 tablespoon honey (optional)
- 1 banana, sliced (optional)

INSTRUCTIONS

1. In a microwave-safe bowl, combine the instant oats and water or milk.
2. Microwave on high for 1-2 minutes until the oats are fully cooked.
3. Stir in the peanut butter and honey if using.
4. Top with banana slices if desired and serve immediately.

Tomato and Red Onion Salad

4

10 Minutes

/

INGREDIENTS

- 4 large tomatoes, sliced
- 1/2 red onion, thinly sliced
- 2 tablespoons olive oil
- 1 tablespoon red wine vinegar
- Salt and pepper, to taste
- Fresh basil leaves for garnish

INSTRUCTIONS

1. Arrange the tomato slices on a serving platter.
2. Top with thinly sliced red onion.
3. Drizzle with olive oil and red wine vinegar.
4. Season with salt and pepper, and garnish with fresh basil leaves.
5. Serve immediately.

Apple Slices with Peanut Butter and Chia Seeds

 2

 5 Minutes

 /

INGREDIENTS

- 2 apples, cored and sliced
- 1/4 cup peanut butter
- 1 tablespoon chia seeds

INSTRUCTIONS

1. Arrange the apple slices on a serving platter.
2. Spread peanut butter on each apple slice.
3. Sprinkle with chia seeds.
4. Serve immediately as a snack or light dessert.

Quick Tomato and Basil Soup

 4

 5 Minutes

20 Minutes

INGREDIENTS

- 2 tablespoons olive oil
- 1 onion, diced
- 3 garlic cloves, minced
- 4 large tomatoes, chopped
- 4 cups vegetable broth
- 1/4 cup fresh basil leaves, chopped
- Salt and pepper, to taste
- 1/4 cup heavy cream (optional)

INSTRUCTIONS

1. Heat olive oil in a large pot over medium heat. Add the onion and cook for 5 minutes until softened.
2. Stir in the garlic and cook for 1 minute until fragrant.
3. Add the chopped tomatoes and vegetable broth. Bring to a simmer and cook for 15 minutes.
4. Stir in the fresh basil and season with salt and pepper.
5. Use an immersion blender to puree the soup until smooth. Stir in the heavy cream if using.
6. Serve hot, garnished with additional basil if desired.

Egg White Frittata with Spinach

2

5 Minutes

10 Minutes

INGREDIENTS

- 6 egg whites
- 1 cup fresh spinach leaves
- 1/4 cup red bell pepper, diced
- 1/4 cup onion, diced
- Salt and pepper, to taste
- 1 tablespoon olive oil

INSTRUCTIONS

1. In a bowl, whisk the egg whites with salt and pepper.
2. Heat olive oil in a non-stick skillet over medium heat. Add the diced onion and red bell pepper, cooking for 3-4 minutes until softened.
3. Add the spinach leaves and cook for 1-2 minutes until wilted.
4. Pour the egg whites over the vegetables in the skillet. Cook without stirring for 3-4 minutes until the edges are set.
5. Carefully flip the frittata and cook for another 2 minutes until fully set.
6. Serve immediately.

Coconut and Pineapple Smoothie

2

5 Minutes

/

INGREDIENTS

- 1 cup coconut milk
- 1 cup fresh or frozen pineapple chunks
- 1/2 banana
- 1 tablespoon honey or maple syrup (optional)
- 1/2 cup ice cubes

INSTRUCTIONS

1. In a blender, combine coconut milk, pineapple chunks, banana, honey or maple syrup (if using), and ice cubes.
2. Blend until smooth and creamy.
3. Pour into glasses and serve immediately.

CHAPTER 11
A 120-DAY MEAL PLAN FOR OPTIMAL HEALTH

WEEK 1

Monday
- **Breakfast:** Green smoothie with spinach and avocado
- **Lunch:** Quinoa salad with avocado, tomatoes, and black beans
- **Dinner:** Fish fillet with grilled vegetables
- **Snack:** Nut and seed energy bars

Tuesday
- **Breakfast:** Almond flour pancakes with berries
- **Lunch:** Lettuce wraps with chicken and hummus
- **Dinner:** Chicken and broccoli stir-fry with brown rice
- **Snack:** Kale chips with sea salt

Wednesday
- **Breakfast:** Scrambled eggs with spinach and avocado
- **Lunch:** Lentil and spinach soup
- **Dinner:** Stuffed eggplant with quinoa and sun-dried tomatoes
- **Snack:** Hummus with carrots and cucumbers

Thursday
- **Breakfast:** Chia seed porridge with almond milk
- **Lunch:** Baked salmon with asparagus and lemon
- **Dinner:** Chicken curry with coconut milk and spinach
- **Snack:** Greek yogurt with dried fruit

Friday
- **Breakfast:** Mushroom and fresh herbs omelette
- **Lunch:** Arugula salad with walnuts, pears, and gorgonzola
- **Dinner:** Pork chops with kale and sweet potatoes
- **Snack:** Fruit and vegetable smoothie

Saturday
- **Breakfast:** Homemade granola with nuts and seeds
- **Lunch:** Buddha bowl with brown rice, vegetables, and tofu
- **Dinner:** Chicken soup with vegetables and ginger

- **Snack:** Homemade popcorn with coconut oil

Sunday
- **Breakfast:** Zucchini and pepper frittata
- **Lunch:** Zoodles (zucchini noodles) with basil pesto
- **Dinner:** Cabbage tacos with shrimp and guacamole
- **Snack:** Trail mix with dark chocolate and nuts

WEEK 2

Monday
- **Breakfast:** Baked egg and vegetable muffins
- **Lunch:** Sweet potato and spinach frittata
- **Dinner:** Miso soup with tofu and mushrooms
- **Snack:** Almond flour muffins with blueberries

Tuesday
- **Breakfast:** Greek yogurt with nuts and honey
- **Lunch:** Tuna salad with avocado and sunflower seeds
- **Dinner:** Turkey meatballs with tomato sauce and vegetables
- **Snack:** Guacamole with sweet potato chips

Wednesday
- **Breakfast:** Whole grain toast with avocado and sesame seeds
- **Lunch:** Grilled chicken with kale and apple salad
- **Dinner:** Stuffed bell peppers with brown rice and black beans
- **Snack:** Cucumber bites with goat cheese

Thursday
- **Breakfast:** Green smoothie with spinach and avocado
- **Lunch:** Chickpea and spinach curry
- **Dinner:** Roasted cauliflower with cheese and herbs
- **Snack:** Berry and almond crumble

Friday
- **Breakfast:** Almond flour pancakes with berries
- **Lunch:** Farro salad with sun-dried tomatoes and olives
- **Dinner:** Chicken and broccoli stir-fry with brown rice
- **Snack:** Nut and seed energy bars

Saturday
- **Breakfast:** Scrambled eggs with spinach and avocado

- **Lunch:** Black bean and corn soup
- **Dinner:** Chicken fajitas with peppers and onions
- **Snack:** Kale chips with sea salt

Sunday
- **Breakfast:** Chia seed porridge with almond milk
- **Lunch:** Bean and quinoa burgers
- **Dinner:** Vegetable curry with coconut milk
- **Snack:** Hummus with carrots and cucumbers

WEEK 3

Monday
- **Breakfast:** Mushroom and fresh herbs omelette
- **Lunch:** Tomato and basil soup
- **Dinner:** Pork tenderloin with roasted cauliflower
- **Snack:** Greek yogurt with dried fruit

Tuesday
- **Breakfast:** Homemade granola with nuts and seeds
- **Lunch:** Stuffed sweet potatoes with avocado and beans
- **Dinner:** Chicken cacciatore with mushrooms
- **Snack:** Fruit and vegetable smoothie

Wednesday
- **Breakfast:** Zucchini and pepper frittata
- **Lunch:** Vegetable and lentil soup
- **Dinner:** Black bean and tomato chili
- **Snack:** Trail mix with dark chocolate and nuts

Thursday
- **Breakfast:** Baked egg and vegetable muffins
- **Lunch:** Lettuce wraps with chicken and hummus
- **Dinner:** Zucchini and meat lasagna
- **Snack:** Almond flour muffins with blueberries

Friday
- **Breakfast:** Greek yogurt with nuts and honey
- **Lunch:** Brown rice salad with vegetables
- **Dinner:** Stuffed bell peppers with brown rice and black beans
- **Snack:** Guacamole with sweet potato chips

Saturday

- **Breakfast:** Whole grain toast with avocado and sesame seeds
- **Lunch:** Chickpea and spinach stew
- **Dinner:** Grilled eggplant with parsley and garlic
- **Snack:** Homemade popcorn with coconut oil

Sunday

- **Breakfast:** Green smoothie with spinach and avocado
- **Lunch:** Cauliflower risotto with mushrooms
- **Dinner:** Turkey meatballs with tomato sauce and vegetables
- **Snack:** Cucumber bites with goat cheese

WEEK 4

Monday

- **Breakfast:** Almond flour pancakes with berries
- **Lunch:** Lentil meatballs with tomato sauce
- **Dinner:** Baked vegetable frittata
- **Snack:** Nut and seed energy bars

Tuesday

- **Breakfast:** Scrambled eggs with spinach and avocado
- **Lunch:** Black bean and corn soup
- **Dinner:** Chicken curry with coconut milk and spinach
- **Snack:** Kale chips with sea salt

Wednesday

- **Breakfast:** Chia seed porridge with almond milk
- **Lunch:** Tomato and basil soup
- **Dinner:** Roasted sweet potatoes with rosemary
- **Snack:** Hummus with carrots and cucumbers

Thursday

- **Breakfast:** Mushroom and fresh herbs omelette
- **Lunch:** Arugula salad with walnuts, pears, and gorgonzola
- **Dinner:** Stuffed eggplant with quinoa and sun-dried tomatoes
- **Snack:** Berry and almond crumble

Friday

- **Breakfast:** Homemade granola with nuts and seeds
- **Lunch:** Buddha bowl with brown rice, vegetables, and tofu

- **Dinner:** Cabbage tacos with shrimp and guacamole
- **Snack:** Almond flour muffins with blueberries

Saturday

- **Breakfast:** Zucchini and pepper frittata
- **Lunch:** Chickpea and spinach curry
- **Dinner:** Chicken and broccoli stir-fry with brown rice
- **Snack:** Fruit and vegetable smoothie

Sunday

- **Breakfast:** Baked egg and vegetable muffins
- **Lunch:** Farro salad with sun-dried tomatoes and olives
- **Dinner:** Black bean and tomato chili
- **Snack:** Guacamole with sweet potato chips

Notes:

- **Rotation:** Each week introduces new recipes from different chapters to keep the menu fresh.
- **Snacks:** Healthy snacks are included to maintain energy levels throughout the day.
- **Prep:** Feel free to adjust meal sizes and portions based on individual needs.

This meal plan provides a balanced and varied approach to eating, ensuring you enjoy a wide range of flavors and nutrients over the four months.

CHAPTER 12
14-DAY DETOX PROGRAM

Preparation:

1. **Plan Your Meals**: Review the entire 14-day plan and purchase all necessary ingredients in advance. Prepping ingredients ahead of time will make meal preparation easier.

2. **Eliminate Processed Foods**: In the week leading up to the detox, begin eliminating processed foods, refined sugars, and artificial sweeteners from your diet.

3. **Sleep and Rest**: Ensure you're getting adequate sleep and managing stress effectively to support the detox process.

Daily Routine:

- **Morning**: Start each morning with warm lemon water, followed by a light stretching routine or yoga to energize your body.

- **Meals**: Follow the meal plan closely. Focus on mindful eating, chewing thoroughly, and savoring each bite.
- **Hydration**: Keep yourself hydrated throughout the day with water, herbal teas, and detoxifying drinks like green tea or dandelion tea.
- **Evening**: Wind down with relaxation exercises or meditation, followed by a herbal tea to promote restful sleep.

14-Day Meal Plan:

Day 1
- **Breakfast**: Green smoothie with spinach and avocado
- **Lunch**: Quinoa salad with avocado, tomatoes, and black beans
- **Dinner**: Chicken and broccoli stir-fry with brown rice
- **Snack**: Kale chips with sea salt

Day 2
- **Breakfast**: Almond flour pancakes with berries
- **Lunch**: Lettuce wraps with chicken and hummus
- **Dinner**: Fish fillet with grilled vegetables
- **Snack**: Hummus with carrots and cucumbers

Day 3
- **Breakfast**: Chia seed porridge with almond milk
- **Lunch**: Lentil and spinach soup
- **Dinner**: Stuffed eggplant with quinoa and sun-dried tomatoes
- **Snack**: Nut and seed energy bars

Day 4
- **Breakfast**: Mushroom and fresh herbs omelette
- **Lunch**: Arugula salad with walnuts, pears, and gorgonzola
- **Dinner**: Chicken soup with vegetables and ginger
- **Snack**: Greek yogurt with dried fruit

Day 5
- **Breakfast**: Homemade granola with nuts and seeds
- **Lunch**: Buddha bowl with brown rice, vegetables, and tofu
- **Dinner**: Chicken curry with coconut milk and spinach
- **Snack**: Fruit and vegetable smoothie

Day 6

- **Breakfast**: Zucchini and pepper frittata
- **Lunch**: Sweet potato and spinach frittata
- **Dinner**: Pork chops with kale and sweet potatoes
- **Snack**: Trail mix with dark chocolate and nuts

Day 7

- **Breakfast**: Greek yogurt with nuts and honey
- **Lunch**: Tuna salad with avocado and sunflower seeds
- **Dinner**: Cabbage tacos with shrimp and guacamole
- **Snack**: Almond flour muffins with blueberries

Day 8

- **Breakfast**: Whole grain toast with avocado and sesame seeds
- **Lunch**: Grilled chicken with kale and apple salad
- **Dinner**: Turkey meatballs with tomato sauce and vegetables
- **Snack**: Cucumber bites with goat cheese

Day 9

- **Breakfast**: Baked egg and vegetable muffins
- **Lunch**: Zoodles (zucchini noodles) with basil pesto
- **Dinner**: Stuffed bell peppers with brown rice and black beans
- **Snack**: Nut and seed energy bars

Day 10

- **Breakfast**: Scrambled eggs with spinach and avocado
- **Lunch**: Lentil and spinach soup
- **Dinner**: Chicken cacciatore with mushrooms
- **Snack**: Kale chips with sea salt

Day 11

- **Breakfast**: Green smoothie with spinach and avocado
- **Lunch**: Quinoa salad with avocado, tomatoes, and black beans
- **Dinner**: Chicken and broccoli stir-fry with brown rice
- **Snack**: Hummus with carrots and cucumbers

Day 12

- **Breakfast**: Almond flour pancakes with berries
- **Lunch**: Farro salad with sun-dried tomatoes and olives
- **Dinner**: Stuffed eggplant with quinoa and sun-dried tomatoes
- **Snack**: Fruit and vegetable smoothie

Day 13

- **Breakfast**: Chia seed porridge with almond milk
- **Lunch**: Black bean and corn soup
- **Dinner**: Chicken curry with coconut milk and spinach
- **Snack**: Homemade popcorn with coconut oil

Day 14

- **Breakfast**: Mushroom and fresh herbs omelette
- **Lunch**: Buddha bowl with brown rice, vegetables, and tofu
- **Dinner**: Fish fillet with grilled vegetables
- **Snack**: Almond flour muffins with blueberries

Maximizing the Benefits:

1. Listen to Your Body: Pay attention to how your body responds to different foods during the detox. Adjust portions and meals based on your hunger and energy levels.

2. Rest and Recovery: Prioritize sleep and relaxation. Your body detoxifies and regenerates during sleep, so aim for 7-8 hours of quality sleep each night.

3. Exercise: Engage in light to moderate exercise, such as walking, yoga, or swimming, to support the detox process without overburdening your body.

4. Stress Management: Incorporate mindfulness practices like meditation, deep breathing, or journaling to help manage stress and enhance the detox process.

5. Avoid Processed Foods: Stick to whole, unprocessed foods during the detox to minimize toxins and maximize nutrient intake.

CHAPTER 13 BONUS
MINDFULNESS AND STRESS REDUCTION EXERCISES AND WEEKLY SHOPPING LISTS

PASSWORD: Avery24

CHAPTER 14
DETAILED SHOPPING LIST

Produce

- **Leafy Greens**
  - ☐ Spinach (fresh, for salads and cooking)
  - ☐ Kale
  - ☐ Arugula
  - ☐ Fresh basil (for salads, pesto, and sauces)
  - ☐ Fresh cilantro (for garnishes and flavoring)
  - ☐ Fresh parsley (for garnishes and cooking)
  - ☐ Fresh mint (optional, for salads and soups)
  - ☐ Fresh dill (for salads and yogurt-based sauces)

- **Vegetables**
  - ☐ Zucchini (for salads, noodles, and frittatas)
  - ☐ Bell peppers (red, green, yellow – for salads, stir-fries, and snacks)
  - ☐ Broccoli (for soups, stir-fries, and side dishes)
  - ☐ Cauliflower (for roasting, risotto, and soups)
  - ☐ Mushrooms (for omelettes, risotto, and stir-fries)
  - ☐ Carrots (for salads, snacks, and stews)
  - ☐ Cucumbers (for salads, tzatziki, and snacks)
  - ☐ Onions (red, yellow, and white – for soups, salads, and stews)
  - ☐ Garlic (for sauces, marinades, and cooking)
  - ☐ Sweet potatoes (for roasting, salads, and frittatas)
  - ☐ Brussels sprouts (for roasting)
  - ☐ Eggplant (for stuffing and grilling)
  - ☐ Cherry tomatoes (for salads, toast, and sauces)
  - ☐ Large tomatoes (for sauces, soups, and salads)
  - ☐ Asparagus (for roasting and salads)
  - ☐ Red cabbage (for tacos and salads)
  - ☐ Celery (for soups, stews, and salads)
  - ☐ Endive (for stuffing with guacamole)

□ Fresh ginger (for soups and curries)

- **Fruits**
  □ Apples (for salads, snacks, and baking)
  □ Bananas (for smoothies and toast)
  □ Berries (strawberries, blueberries, raspberries – for smoothies, salads, and desserts)
  □ Avocados (for salads, toast, guacamole, and smoothies)
  □ Lemons and limes (for dressings, marinades, and beverages)
  □ Pears (for salads)
  □ Pineapple (for smoothies)
  □ Grapes (for fruit salads and snacks)

Pantry Staples

- **Grains**
  □ Whole grain bread (for toast)
  □ Whole grain oats (instant and rolled, for oatmeal and baking)
  □ Brown rice (for salads and side dishes)
  □ Quinoa (for salads and side dishes)
  □ Farro (for salads)
  □ Almond flour (for pancakes, muffins, and baking)
  □ Whole grain or gluten-free pasta (optional, for lasagna and side dishes)

- **Legumes**
  □ Canned chickpeas (for salads, soups, and curries)
  □ Canned black beans (for soups, salads, and burgers)
  □ Canned kidney beans (for chili)
  □ Lentils (dry or canned, for soups and stews)
  □ Canned or cooked white beans (optional, for soups and salads)

- **Nuts and Seeds**
  □ Almonds (whole and sliced, for snacks, salads, and baking)
  □ Walnuts (for salads and baking)
  □ Sunflower seeds (for salads and snacks)
  □ Pumpkin seeds (for granola and snacks)
  □ Chia seeds (for porridge and snacks)

- ☐ Flaxseeds (ground, for yogurt and baking)
- ☐ Hemp seeds (for smoothies and salads)

- **Oils and Fats**
  - ☐ Olive oil (extra virgin, for cooking and dressings)
  - ☐ Coconut oil (for cooking, baking, and popcorn)
  - ☐ Sesame oil (for stir-fries and marinades)
  - ☐ Nut butters (almond butter, peanut butter – for snacks and baking)
  - ☐ Tahini (for dressings and sauces)

- **Condiments and Spices**
  - ☐ Honey or maple syrup (for baking and sweetening)
  - ☐ Dijon mustard (for dressings and marinades)
  - ☐ Balsamic vinegar (for salads and dressings)
  - ☐ Red wine vinegar (for salads)
  - ☐ Apple cider vinegar (for dressings and cooking)
  - ☐ Soy sauce or tamari (for stir-fries and marinades)
  - ☐ Miso paste (for soups and sauces)
  - ☐ Curry powder (for curries and stews)
  - ☐ Ground cumin (for soups, stews, and chili)
  - ☐ Smoked paprika (for soups, stews, and seasoning)
  - ☐ Ground turmeric (for curries and stews)
  - ☐ Dried oregano (for sauces and seasoning)
  - ☐ Dried basil (for sauces and seasoning)
  - ☐ Dried thyme (for soups, stews, and roasts)
  - ☐ Ground cinnamon (for baking and oatmeal)
  - ☐ Ground ginger (optional, for baking and cooking)
  - ☐ Garlic powder (for seasoning and cooking)
  - ☐ Onion powder (for seasoning and cooking)
  - ☐ Sea salt and black pepper (for seasoning)
  - ☐ Red pepper flakes (optional, for heat and seasoning)

Protein

- **Animal-Based Proteins**
  - ☐ Boneless, skinless chicken breasts (for stir-fries, salads, and soups)

- ☐ Chicken thighs (for cacciatore and curries)
- ☐ Ground turkey (for meatballs and burgers)
- ☐ Pork tenderloin or pork chops (for roasts and main dishes)
- ☐ Salmon fillets (for baking and salads)
- ☐ White fish fillets (for grilling and main dishes)
- ☐ Eggs (large, for breakfast dishes and baking)
- ☐ Greek yogurt (plain, for snacks, smoothies, and baking)
- ☐ Hard-boiled eggs (for snacks and salads)
- ☐ Feta, mozzarella, and Parmesan cheese (for salads, frittatas, and baking)
- ☐ Gorgonzola cheese (for salads)

- **Plant-Based Proteins**
  - ☐ Tofu (for stir-fries and soups)
  - ☐ Tempeh (optional, for plant-based protein in salads and stir-fries)
  - ☐ Plant-based protein powder (optional, for smoothies and snacks)

Baking Essentials
- **Flours**
  - ☐ Almond flour (for baking and pancakes)
  - ☐ Coconut flour (optional, for baking)

- **Sweeteners**
  - ☐ Honey or maple syrup (for baking and sweetening)
  - ☐ Coconut sugar (optional, for baking)
  - ☐ Dark chocolate chips (for baking and snacks)

- **Baking Add-ins**
  - ☐ Baking powder and baking soda (for baking)
  - ☐ Vanilla extract (for baking and smoothies)
  - ☐ Cocoa powder (for baking and smoothies)
  - ☐ Shredded coconut (optional, for baking and snacks)

Frozen Items
- **Fruits and Vegetables**
  - ☐ Frozen berries (for smoothies and baking)

- ☐ Frozen spinach (for smoothies and cooking)
- ☐ Frozen peas (for soups and cooking)

Beverages
- **Non-Dairy Milks**
  - ☐ Unsweetened almond milk (for smoothies, porridge, and baking)
  - ☐ Coconut milk (canned, for curries and soups)

- **Teas**
  - ☐ Matcha powder (for smoothies and beverages)
  - ☐ Herbal teas (optional, for calming and digestive support)

Specialty Items
- **Snacks**
  - ☐ Dark chocolate bars (for snacking and baking)
  - ☐ Plant-based protein bars (optional, for on-the-go snacks)

- **Miscellaneous**
  - ☐ Parchment paper (for baking and roasting)
  - ☐ Storage containers (for meal prepping and storing leftovers)
  - ☐ Reusable produce bags (for storing fresh produce)

Make-Ahead Staples
- **Batch Cooking**
  - ☐ Quinoa (cook in bulk for use in salads and side dishes)
  - ☐ Brown rice (cook in bulk for use in salads and side dishes)
  - ☐ Lentils (cook in bulk for soups and stews)
  - ☐ Homemade granola (make a large batch for breakfasts and snacks)

This shopping list is designed to help you stock your kitchen with the essentials needed to create healthy, healing meals over the next four months. Adjust quantities based on your household size and meal preferences.

CONCLUSION

As you reach the conclusion of this cookbook, it's important to reflect on the journey you've taken toward better metabolic health. This book has provided you with a comprehensive understanding of how food directly impacts your body's ability to maintain balanced blood sugar levels, sustain energy, and support overall well-being. By embracing the principles of metabolic cooking, you are not just adopting a diet; you are making a long-term commitment to your health.

Metabolic health is the foundation of a vibrant and fulfilling life. It influences everything from how you feel throughout the day to your long-term risk of developing chronic diseases. By prioritizing meals that are rich in whole, nutrient-dense foods, you've taken significant steps toward ensuring that your body operates at its best. The recipes and meal plans in this book are designed to be both practical and enjoyable, demonstrating that eating for health doesn't mean sacrificing flavor or satisfaction.

The conclusion is not an end, but rather the beginning of a new chapter in your life. The knowledge and habits you've cultivated here are tools that will serve you well beyond the pages of this book. Whether you're cooking for yourself or your family, the choices you make in the kitchen will have lasting impacts on your health.

As you move forward, remember that consistency is key. Healthy eating is not about perfection, but about making better choices more often. Continue to experiment with recipes, explore new ingredients, and listen to your body's needs. The path to optimal health is a journey, and with the right mindset and tools, it is one that you can enjoy every step of the way.

Tips for Continuing Healthy Eating

Maintaining the progress you've made towards better metabolic health requires ongoing commitment and a few practical strategies. As you move beyond the initial phase of adopting these recipes and habits, it's crucial to establish a sustainable routine that keeps you on track while allowing for flexibility and enjoyment.

1. **Plan Ahead:** One of the most effective ways to ensure you stick to healthy eating habits is through planning. Set aside time each week to plan your meals, make a grocery list, and prepare ingredients in advance. Meal prepping can save time during busy weekdays and reduces the temptation to reach for less healthy convenience foods.

2. **Stay Hydrated:** Proper hydration is key to supporting your metabolism and overall health. Start your day with a glass of water, and aim to drink regularly throughout the day. Herbal teas and infused waters are great alternatives to sugary drinks and can help keep you hydrated while adding variety to your routine.

3. **Embrace Variety:** Eating the same foods repeatedly can lead to nutrient gaps and food fatigue. Keep your meals exciting by experimenting with different ingredients, trying new recipes, and incorporating seasonal produce. This not only ensures a wide range of nutrients but also keeps your meals interesting and satisfying.

4. **Listen to Your Body:** As you continue on your journey, pay attention to how different foods make you feel. Everyone's body is unique, and what works for one person might not work

for another. Adjust your meals based on your energy levels, digestion, and overall well-being.

5. **Practice Mindful Eating:** Take time to savor your meals without distractions. Eating mindfully helps you enjoy your food more and recognize when you're full, preventing overeating and promoting a healthy relationship with food.

By integrating these tips into your daily life, you can maintain the benefits of metabolic cooking and continue to support your health for the long term.

How to Adapt Recipes to Your Needs

Every individual has unique nutritional needs, preferences, and goals, making it important to learn how to adapt recipes to suit your specific circumstances. The recipes in this book are designed with metabolic health in mind, but with a few simple adjustments, they can be tailored even further to fit your dietary requirements, whether you're managing a specific health condition, catering to food sensitivities, or simply aiming to meet personal taste preferences.

1. **Adjusting Macronutrients:** If you're following a specific macronutrient ratio, such as a higher protein or lower carbohydrate intake, it's easy to modify recipes to fit your goals. For example, you can increase the protein content of a meal by adding extra lean meats, tofu, or legumes. To reduce carbs, swap out starchy vegetables or grains for low-carb alternatives like cauliflower rice or zucchini noodles.

2. **Accommodating Food Allergies and Sensitivities:** For those with food allergies or intolerances, most recipes can be adjusted to exclude problematic ingredients. Common swaps include using almond or coconut flour instead of wheat flour for gluten-free cooking, or replacing dairy with plant-based alternatives like almond milk, coconut yogurt, or nutritional yeast.

3. **Enhancing Nutrient Density:** To boost the nutritional profile of a recipe, consider adding extra vegetables, seeds, or nuts. Leafy greens, for instance, can be easily incorporated into smoothies, omelettes, or soups, while seeds like chia or flax can be sprinkled on top of dishes for added fiber and omega-3 fatty acids.

4. **Catering to Taste Preferences:** Everyone's palate is different, so feel free to experiment with spices, herbs, and seasoning levels to suit your tastes. If you prefer spicier food, add more chili or pepper to dishes, or if you like sweeter flavors, consider natural sweeteners like honey or maple syrup in moderation.

5. **Scaling Recipes:** Depending on your situation, you might need to scale recipes up or down. If you're cooking for one, halving recipes can prevent waste. Conversely, doubling recipes can be a time-saver for families or for meal prepping.

By understanding how to adapt recipes, you empower yourself to take full control of your diet, ensuring that every meal not only supports your metabolic health but also fits seamlessly into your lifestyle and preferences.

Resources for Further Reading and Study

As you continue your journey toward better metabolic health, expanding your knowledge through further reading and study can empower you to make more informed choices and deepen your understanding of the connection between diet and health. This section provides a curated list of resources that can help you explore various aspects of metabolic health, nutrition, and cooking in greater detail.

1. Books on Metabolic Health:

Several books delve into the science of metabolic health, offering insights into how diet, lifestyle, and genetics influence your metabolism. Some recommended titles include:

- *"The Obesity Code" by Dr. Jason Fung:* This book explains the role of insulin in weight gain and offers practical advice on how to manage insulin levels through diet.

- *"Metabolical" by Dr. Robert Lustig:* A deep dive into how food processing affects our metabolism and overall health, and what we can do to combat these effects.

- *"The Diabetes Code" by Dr. Jason Fung:* Focused on reversing type 2 diabetes, this book explores the impact of diet on blood sugar and insulin.

2. Scientific Journals and Articles:

For those interested in exploring the latest research, academic journals such as *"The American Journal of Clinical Nutrition"* and *"Diabetes Care"* offer peer-reviewed studies on topics related to nutrition, metabolism, and chronic diseases. Reading these can provide a deeper understanding of how ongoing research informs dietary recommendations.

3. Online Courses and Webinars:

Platforms like Coursera, edX, and Khan Academy offer courses on nutrition, dietetics, and metabolic health. These can be a great way to gain structured learning and a more formal understanding of the subject.

4. Reputable Websites and Blogs:

Websites such as *"Harvard Health Publishing"*, *"Mayo Clinic"*, and *"NutritionFacts.org"* provide reliable, evidence-based information on various health topics. These sites are excellent for keeping up with new research findings and practical health tips.

5. Documentaries and Podcasts:

Visual and audio content can also be a valuable way to learn. Documentaries like *"Fed Up"* and *"The Magic Pill"* explore the effects of diet on health, while podcasts such as *"The Doctor's Farmacy"* by Dr. Mark Hyman discuss metabolic health with experts from various fields.

By engaging with these resources, you can continue to build on the foundation laid by this cookbook, equipping yourself with the knowledge to make lasting, positive changes to your health.

Made in the USA
Las Vegas, NV
09 September 2024

94979617R00050